SECUNDAR

You!

Ramón Palencia

Liz Driscoll

with
María Jesús Cumming

2

Students' Book

LONGMAN

UNIT	FINAL TASK	FUNCTIONS
1 Introduction · 1	**REVISION**	
2 Countries · 5	• Writing or recording ten facts about a country. • Reading or listening to ten facts about a country and identifying the country.	Comparing places: *France is larger than Spain.* Talking about countries - location, size, population, languages, capital, geography, etc: *Tanzania is in the east of Africa.* *What's the population of Canada?*
3 My Town · 13	• Preparing an information pack about your town.	Talking about location: *The car park is under the Old Market.* Describing places: *Mr Mario's is a restaurant where you can make your own pizzas. There's an aquarium at Golden Gate Park.*
4 Keep Fit · 21	• Giving instructions for an exercise routine. • Carrying out instructions for an exercise routine.	Giving instructions: *Stand with your feet apart.* *Raise your right arm slowly.*
5 Time Out · 29	**CONSOLIDATION Units 2-4**	**LEARNING TO LEARN Listening; Speaking**
6 Your Stars · 35	• Writing a horoscope with predictions for next weekend. • Reading a horoscope and reporting on the predictions after the weekend.	Expressing certainty: *You will / won't have a good w* Expressing uncertainty: *You might (not) go to Ameri* Asking about the future: *Will I be rich?* Reporting: *The horoscope said I would pass my exa*
7 Sports Mad · 43	• Designing a new game and explaining it to the class. • Voting for the wackiest/most practical games and playing them.	Talking and asking about routine obligations: *You ha* *pass the ball to each other. Do you have to kick the* Talking and asking about actions which are permitte* *not permitted: You can carry the ball in your hands. You can't bounce the ball.*
8 Famous People · 53	• Preparing questions for a quiz about famous people from the past. • Taking part in a quiz about famous people from the past.	Talking about the past: *Agatha Christie was a famous writer.* Asking about the past: *Who wrote Huckleberry Finn? When did Alexander Fleming die? Did he design the Sagrada,Familia?*
9 Time Out · 61	**CONSOLIDATION Units 6-8**	**LEARNING TO LEARN Reading; Writing**
10 School Rules · 67	• Writing rules for your school. • Agreeing on ten rules for teachers and ten rules for students.	Expressing obligation: *You must have a good breakf* Expressing prohibition: *You mustn't eat sweets.* Expressing lack of obligation: *You don't have to go every day.* Giving reasons: *I don't like uniforms because ...*
11 Boys and Girls · 75	• Taking part in a class debate about the similarities and differences between girls and boys.	Comparing: *Girls are more / less hard-working than* Giving opinions: *I think …* Agreeing / Disagreeing: *I agree / don't agree / disag* Giving arguments: *Most women don't like war.* Talking about ability: *I'm good at running.*
12 Tourists · 83	• Interviewing tourists about the places they have visited and their opinions of your country. • Writing the results of your interviews and making a poster to display the results.	Talking about recent experiences: *We've been to Yo* Asking about recent experiences: *Have you met many British people?* Asking for and giving opinions: *What do you think of Britain? I think it's a beautiful c*
13 Time Out · 91	**CONSOLIDATION Units 10-12**	**LEARNING TO LEARN Guessing the meaning of new words; English around you**
14 Break in · 97	• Preparing an alibi with two classmates. • Checking other students' alibis.	Talking and asking about situations at specific times in the past: *At 9 o'clock last Sunday I was sleeping.* *were you doing at 10 am last Saturday? I was study.* Reporting: *He says a girl was flying an aeroplane.* Talking about possession: *Whose CD is this? It's mir*
15 Once upon a time … · 105	• Writing a modern version of a traditional story. • Reading other people's stories and matching them with the original. • Voting for your favourite story.	Narrating: *Once upon a time there was a …* Establishing the sequence of events: *One day the Queen died.* *That evening there was a knock at the door.*
16 Time Out · 113	**CONSOLIDATION Units 14-15**	**LEARNING TO LEARN Talking to yourself**

GRAMMAR	PRONUNCIATION	VOCABULARY
omparative and superlative adjectives: *-er, -est* *nger / more important than ...* *e longest / the most important ... in ...* ardinal numbers	Sentence Rhythm	Geographical features: *archipelago,* *continent, city, mountain, river ...* Countries Languages High numbers: *3,450,000*
elative pronouns: *that, where* repositions of place ecycling of *there is / are* and *can*	Sentence Rhythm	Places in towns and cities: *railway station, car park, hotel, theatre,* *cinema, church, castle, restaurant ...*
mperative: affirmative and negative dverbs of direction (*up / down, forwards / backwards,* *ght / left*) and manner (*quickly, slowly, carefully, gently*)	Sentence Rhythm	Parts of the body Action verbs : *bend, stretch, stand ...*

EVISION A game: Travelling

GRAMMAR	PRONUNCIATION	VOCABULARY
ill / won't / might / might not* uestions and short answers with *will* eported speech: *will / won't* ➔ *would / wouldn't*	Contractions: *'ll, won't*	Dates Signs of the Zodiac
ave to: affirmative, questions and short answers* *an:* affirmative, negative, questions and ort answers npersonal *you* bject pronouns: *it*	Sentence Rhythm	Games Sports equipment Transitive action verbs: *pass, hit* *bounce ...*
ast simple: subject and object questions with *h*-words - *Who, What, Where, When,* and *Which* ecycling of *Yes / No* questions with *Did* and *Was*	*-ed* ending: /d/, /t/. and /ɪd/	Occupations and related words: *architect / design, artist / paint ...* Inventions and discoveries: *vaccination, dynamite ...*

VISION A game: People in History

GRAMMAR	PRONUNCIATION	VOCABULARY
ust / mustn't / don't have to* ecycling of *have to* and *can / can't*	*must* /mʌs/, /mʌst/ *mustn't* /mʌsən/, /mʌsənt/	School rules Places in a school
omparison of adjectives: *less ... than,* *ot) as ... as, better / worse than* ecycling of *(strong)er / more (mature) than* nd *have to / don't have to*	Sentence Rhythm	Jobs: *airline pilot, engineer ...* Personal qualities: *hard-working,* *honest ...* Household chores: *make the bed,* *wash up ...*
resent perfect: affirmative, negative, uestions and short answers ecycling of present simple	Sentence Rhythm	Countries Nationalities Adjectives describing landscapes, people, food and the weather

VISION A game: Three in a row

GRAMMAR	PRONUNCIATION	VOCABULARY
ast continuous: affirmative, negative, questions nd short answers *hose ...?* /possessive pronouns and *'s* ecycling of *was / were* and past simple	Sentence Rhythm	Times of the day Everyday activities
ast continuous and past simple aid/told equencers	*-ed* ending: /d/, /t/ and /ɪd/	Fairy stories and related vocabulary: *dragon, flying carpet, witch ...* Personal qualities: *beautiful,* *clever, cruel ...*

VISION A game: Noughts and crosses

Welcome to *You! Book 2*. In this introductory unit you have activities to help you remember what you did in *You! Book 1* and to check how much English you know!

VOCABULARY REVISION

1 a Odd-one-out. Which word does not belong in each group? Why not? Tell a classmate.

1 cat, hamster, sister, snake, tortoise
2 beard, eyes, hair, hat, mouth
3 History, French, Library, PE, RE
4 baker, cashier, hamburger, photographer, waiter
5 elephant, giraffe, lion, llama, rhino
6 tracksuit, trainers, tree, T-shirt, trunks

66 Sister. She's not a pet. 99

b Work with a partner. Prepare some odd-one-out series for your classmates.

2 a Match the verbs and the nouns. Then check with your partner.

brush	motorbikes
do	beer
drink	breakfast
go	chess
have	friends
meet	your homework
play	letters
repair	swimming
watch	your teeth
wear	television
write	a uniform

b Which other nouns can you use with the verbs above? Write a list. Then show your list to your partner. Who has the most nouns?

3 a Look at the topics in the box. Can you think of examples for each one? You have a maximum of three minutes to write all the examples down.

One pet
Two parts of the face
Three school subjects
Four school rooms
Five jobs
Six hobbies
Seven names of animals
Eight action verbs

b Compare your lists in groups. Do you understand all the words in your classmates' lists?

How did you do in the vocabulary activities? Did you do ...
a) **very well? Excellent!**
b) **all right? Read your Vocabulary Notebook.**
c) **not very well? Revise the vocabulary in *Book 1*. Use your Vocabulary Notebook.**

4

a Work in pairs. Choose the correct alternative and say what is wrong with the other.
1 I've got/I'm fourteen years old.
2 John is/are from Manchester.
3 Have got you/Have you got any brothers?
4 How old they are/are they?
5 There is/are two gyms in my school.
6 I go/goes to school by bus.
7 I go not/don't go to bed very late.
8 My sister teach/teaches English in Italy.
9 She doesn't live/doesn't lives in England.
10 The giraffes/Giraffes eat leaves from trees.
11 I like read/reading a lot.
12 Last Sunday I goed/went to the cinema.
I see/saw a very interesting film.
13 I was/were really thirsty, so I have/had a large Coke.
14 The Ancient Egyptians didn't play/didn't played basketball.
15 Next Sunday we go/are going to have a picnic in a park.

b Check with another pair.

❝ You don't say 'I go not'.
You say 'I don't go'. ❞

❝ Do you say 'She doesn't live'
or 'She doesn't lives'? ❞

5

Complete the sentences and do the crossword. Then check with your partner.
Clues
Across:
1 I _____ swimming in the sea.
3 What _____ you do yesterday?
5 His mother is _____ doctor.
6 Is Pam _____ sister?
7 There are two bottles _____ the table.
9 _____ there a gym on the ground floor?
10 _____ she got any pets?
11 I _____ an excellent film on Sunday.
13 My brother is _____ actor.
14 Where _____ Tim live?
17 The Ancient Egyptians _____ meat.
18 I _____ to Italy last summer.
19 Jim goes to school _____ bus.
20 There are _____ computers in my classroom.

Down:
2 Look. That's _____ mother.
3 John's brother _____ a taxi.
4 _____ you like reading?
8 Emus _____ swim very well.
10 I was thirsty, so I _____ a coke.
12 Where _____ you yesterday?
15 They _____ up late last Sunday.
16 Last Saturday I _____ some friends.
17 Are there _____ squash courts in your school?
18 I _____ at home yesterday.

How did you do in the grammar activities?
Did you do ...
a) very well? Excellent!
b) all right? Read your Grammar Notebook.
c) not very well? Use your Workbook and your Grammar Notebook to revise.

LISTENING

6 a 📼 **Listen to three conversations. What are the speakers talking about in each one? Match the conversations with the topics in the box. Then check with the class.**

> physical description   free time
> plans for the weekend   personal information
> school   everyday routine   past activities

Mary Parker
27, Lancaster Gardens
Richmond-on-Thames
Surrey
ENGLAND

b 📼 **Listen again and answer the questions. Then check with the class.**
1 Where did John go on Saturday?
2 What is Craig going to do next weekend?
3 What have they got after break?
4 Where's Sandra from?
5 What colour is Sandra's hair?
6 Where does Isabel usually have lunch?
7 How often does she go to the gym?

How did you do with the recordings? Did you do ...
a) **very well? Excellent!**
b) **all right? Pay more attention to listening tasks in class.**
c) **not very well? Pay attention in class and listen to your Workbook Cassette at home.**

SPEAKING

7 a You are going to play a board game. Look at the topics in the squares. What can you say about the topics in English? Do you need time to prepare? You can do this with a partner.

b These are the instructions for the game.
This is a game for two, three or four players.
Each player starts from a different START square.

The winner is the first player to get to the opposite START square. You can move only one square at a time, like this:

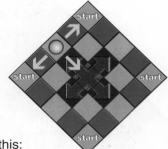

You can't move like this:

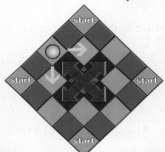

When you land on a square, say something about the topic. If you can't say anything, go back to the previous square.

You can say a little or a lot about each topic. But this is a game to see how much you can remember. Try to say as much as you can.

When someone wins the game, change to new START squares and play a new round.

start

GAME

start

something you like doing

something you did yesterday

something you didn't do yesterday

your favourite school subject

something the Ancient Egyptians did

something the Ancient Egyptians didn't do

something the Ancient Egyptians had

something the Ancient Egyptians didn't have

your family

start

something you do every day

something you do on Sundays

something you never do

start

your plans for next weekend

your friends

your pet

a description of yourself

your school

a local celebrity

a wild animal

your free time

something you did in the summer

start

How did you do in the game?
Did you do ...
a) very well? Excellent!
b) all right? Good!
c) not very well? Practise with a friend.
   Then play the game again.

Countries

②

In this unit you are going to talk about countries of the world. At the end of the unit you will be able to:

- write or record a list of ten facts about a country
- read or listen to ten facts about a country and say which country it is

Now study the final task on page 12.

LET'S GET STARTED

1

a 🔲 **Listen to the words in the box. Do you know their meaning? Work in pairs. Check with a classmate and find examples on the map.**

archipelago	border	city	continent	country
forest	island	lake	mountain	waterfall
mountain range	ocean	river	sea	volcano

b Now tell the class.

❝ I think number 1 is a/an … ❞

c Look at the adjectives in the box. Do you know their pronunciation and their meaning? Ask your partner or your teacher if you don't.

| cold | high | large | long | low | short | small | warm |

d Which adjectives can you use to describe the words in 1a?

❝ A high mountain. ❞

2

a Match the countries with their languages.

| Argentina | Australia | Brazil | France | Greece |
| India | Japan | Kenya | Morocco | Russia |

| Arabic | English | French | Greek | Japanese |
| Hindi | Portuguese | Russian | Spanish | Swahili |

b Work in pairs. Tell your partner.

❝ I think they speak Portuguese in Brazil. ❞

c 🔲 Listen and check.

d Do you know the names of other countries and languages in English? Make a list. Show your list to your partner. Who has more countries for each continent?

How can you learn the new words? Suggest activities or ask your teacher for ideas.

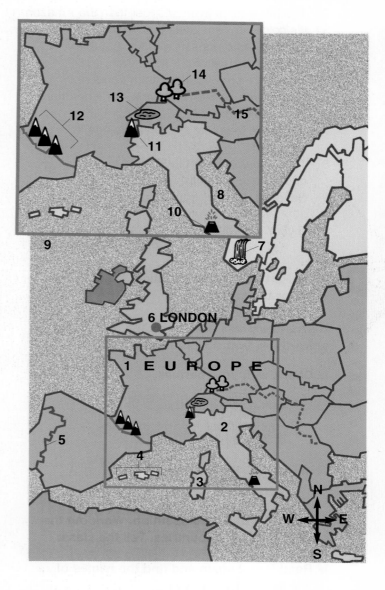

Africa	Asia	America	Europe	Oceania

WIN a fabulous holiday for two in Belize!

Part 1

Are these sentences true or false?

1 France is larger than Spain.
2 The Mississippi river is longer than the Amazon.
3 It's colder in Venezuela than in Finland.
4 Spain is more popular with tourists than Denmark or Sweden.
5 Tokyo is more populated than London.
6 Pico Veleta, in Sierra Nevada, is higher than Mont Blanc in the Alps.
7 English is the most spoken language in the world.
8 The Atacama desert in South America is the driest place on earth.
9 Baseball is the most popular sport in Japan.

Send your answers to: BELIZE HOLIDAY
                         PO Box 7

3 **a Do Part 1 of the competition. Write *true* or *false* for the sentences.**

Remember: ask your teacher if there is something you don't understand.

b Check with your partner.

❝I think number 1 is true.❞

❝Yes, I think it's true.❞

❝I don't think so. I think it's false.❞

4 **a Do Part 2 of the competition. Work out the names of the two countries. Tell the class.**

b Read Part 2 again and find the names of ...
1 the longest river in Asia
2 the world's most populated country
3 the world's highest mountain
4 two Asian cities
5 five Asian countries
6 two South American rivers
7 a South American volcano
8 a South American currency
9 two South American languages
10 an old South American civilisation

Part 2

Can you work out the names of these countries?

"Ni hao! My name's Tip Si. These ten facts are about my country. Do you know where I'm from?"

*   It's the second largest country in Asia and the third largest country in the world.
*   It's the most populated country in the world.
*   People speak many different languages, but the main language is Mandarin.
*   The currency is the Yuan and the flag is red with five yellow stars.
*   Its capital is Beijing. Shanghai is the second most important city.
*   It has several important rivers. The Chang Jiang (5550 km) is the longest river in Asia.
*   Mount Everest (8848 m), on its border with Nepal, is the world's highest mountain.
*   The most interesting places to visit are The Great Wall (2400 km long) and the Forbidden City in Beijing.
*   It has borders with thirteen countries, including Mongolia and Russia in the north, and Pakistan, India and Nepal in the south.
*   The most popular game is table tennis - there are tables in the streets of every village.

Mount Everest is the world's highest mountain.

"¡Hola! My name's Jorge. Can you guess where I come from?"

* This country is the third largest country in South America.
* It has a population of over twenty-two million.
* The main language is Spanish, but in some parts of the Andes people speak Quechua.
* The capital is Lima. Trujillo, in the north, is the second most important town.
* The currency is the 'new sol' and the flag has red and white stripes.
* It has borders with Ecuador, Colombia, Brazil, Bolivia and Chile.
* The highest mountain is Mount Huascarán (6768 m) in the Andes range. It's an extinct volcano. The Andes (7200 km) is the world's longest mountain range.
* The Ucayli is the longest river (1465 km). The Amazon River starts in this country and it flows through the Amazon forest into Brazil and the Atlantic Ocean.
* Lake Titicaca, on the border with Bolivia, is the largest lake in the region (8340 m^2) and the highest navigable lake in the world. The local Indians use a special type of boat for fishing.
* The most famous landmark is the ruin of Machu Picchu, an old Incan fortress in the Andes. The Incas were one of the most advanced civilisations in America.

IN YOUR OWN WORDS

In the competition you can find useful ways of comparing places and things.

A COMPARATIVE

Find these comparisons in Part 1 of the competition.
1 The Mississippi/The Amazon (long)
2 France/Spain (large)

3 Spain/Denmark (popular with tourists)
4 Tokyo/London (populated)

What happens to the adjectives in sentences 1 and 2? What happens to the adjectives in sentences 3 and 4? Why? How do you make comparisons in your language?

Find more examples in the text.

B SUPERLATIVE

Find these sentences in Part 2 of the competition and complete them.
1 Mount Everest is the world's _____ mountain.
2 The Chang Jiang is the _____ river in Asia.

3 The Incas were one of the _____ civilisations in America.
4 Trujillo is the second _____ town.

What happens to the adjectives in sentences 1 and 2? What happens to the adjectives in sentences 3 and 4? Why? How do you form the superlative in your language?

Find more examples in the text.

When do you use the comparative? When do you use the superlative?

5 **a** **Are you good at learning facts? Match these sentences with names in the fact files.**
1 This country is larger than Canada.
2 It's the third most populated country in the world.
3 This river is longer than the Yenisei, but shorter than the Chang Jiang.
4 It's the second highest mountain in the world.
5 It's the fifth smallest country in the world.
6 It's the second most spoken language in the world.

REMEMBER	
the first	the sixth
the second	the seventh
the third	the eighth
the fourth	the ninth
the fifth	the tenth

b **Write sentences like those in 5a and exchange them with a classmate. Match your partner's sentences with names in the fact files.**

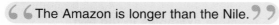
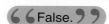

This mountain is lower than the Kanchenjunga but higher than the Dhaulagiri.

c **Check with your partner.**

d **Have you learned the facts? Close your books and test your partner.**

66 The Amazon is longer than the Nile. 99

66 False. 99

HOW DO YOU SAY IT?
Sentence Rhythm

a 🔲 **Listen and repeat. Pay attention to the stress.**
1 Spain's larger than Italy.
2 Italy is more populated than Greece.
3 Russia is the largest country in the world.
4 China is the most populated country.

b 🔲 **Mark the stress. Listen and check.**
1 The Tagus is the longest river in Spain.
2 The Amazon is longer than the Nile.
3 Chinese is the most spoken language in the world.
4 Beijing is more important than Shanghai.

THE 5 MOST POPULATED COUNTRIES

	million people
China	1,130,000
India	860,000
USA	255,000
Indonesia	190,000
Brazil	152,000

THE 5 MOST SPOKEN LANGUAGES

	million people
Chinese	750
English	400
Spanish	300
Russian	265
Hindi	230

THE 5 LONGEST RIVERS

	kilometres
Nile (Africa)	6695
Amazon (S. America)	6440
Chang Jiang (China)	6380
Mississippi (USA)	5970
Yenisei (Russia)	5540

THE 5 SMALLEST COUNTRIES

	square kms
Vatican City	0.4
Monaco	2
Nauru	21
Tuvalu	26
San Marino	61

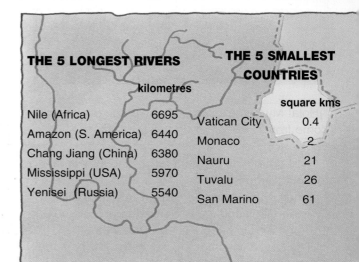

THE 5 HIGHEST MOUNTAINS

	metres
Everest (Nepal/Tibet)	8848
K2 (Godwin Austen) (Pakistan/India)	8611
Kanchenjunga (Nepal/India)	8597
Makalu (Nepal/Tibet)	8480
Dhaulagiri (Nepal)	8169

THE 5 LARGEST COUNTRIES

	square kms
Russia	17,075,000
Canada	9,976,000
China	9,597,000
USA	9,363,000
Brazil	8,512,000

LOOK AND LEARN
longer **than** ...
the longest ... **in** ...

6

a Here's another chance to learn facts. Match these sentences with names in the fact files.

1 This country is in the east of Africa.
2 It's the capital of Tanzania.
3 The currency of this country is the dollar.
4 It's the most famous landmark in Toronto.
5 In this country people speak Swahili.
6 You can see beautiful pagodas in this place.
7 This country is famous for its national parks.
8 This country has a population of a hundred and twenty-five million.
9 It's the longest river in Japan.

b Write 5 - 10 sentences like those in 6a. Exchange them with a classmate. Match your partner's sentences with names in the fact file.

c Check with your partner.

Do you need more practice? Do the activity again with another partner.

LOOK AND LEARN	
1,000	a thousand
2,000	two thousand
100,000	a hundred thousand
1,000,000	a million
2,000,000	two million
3,450,000	three million, four hundred and fifty thousand

Name: Japan
Situation: eastern Asia, in the Pacific Ocean
Area: 377,835 km²
Population: 125,000,000 (the world's seventh largest)
Capital: Tokyo
Language: Japanese
Currency: yen
Highest point: Mount Fuji (3776m)
Longest river: River Tone (322 km)
Other information: Japan is an archipelago with 3922 islands; Honshu is the largest.
There are about 54 active volcanoes in the country.
Tokyo and Yokohama are the world's most populated cities.
Rice and fish are the two most important types of food.
Places to visit: Horyu Temple, with beautiful pagodas.
Kyoto, the old capital, with beautiful temples and gardens.

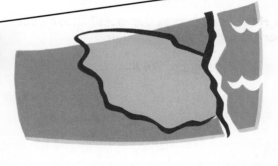

Name: Tanzania
Situation: eastern Africa on the Indian coast
Area: 945,000 km²
Population: 25,000,000
Capital: Dodoma
Languages: English, Swahili
Currency: Tanzanian shilling
Highest point: Mount Kilimanjaro (5895m), the highest mountain in Africa
Longest river: River Rufiji
Other information: Dar es Salaam, on the Indian Ocean, is the most important city.
The Masai, the tallest people in world, live in the north.
Places to visit: The Ngorongoro wildlife reserve, with elephants, lions, giraffes, zebras and many other wild animals, and Lake Victoria, the largest lake in Africa.

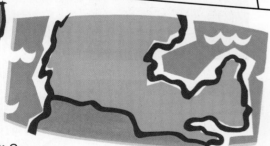

Name: Canada
Situation: northern North America
Area: 9,976,000 km²
Population: 27,000,000
Capital: Ottawa
Languages: English and French
Currency: Canadian dollar
Highest point: Mount Logan (5951 m)
Longest river: The Mackenzie (4241 km)
Other information: Toronto is the largest city; it has the tallest building in the world, the CN Tower (553 m).
It is so cold in winter that children can play ice hockey in the street.
Places to visit: Canada is famous for its National Parks, with lots of forests. The Great Lakes, the world's largest group of lakes, and the Niagara Falls, are on the border with the USA.

STEP BY STEP

7 **a** 📼 The students at a school in Bangalore have recorded 'Ten Facts about India'. Look at the words below. What do the speakers say about each of them?

Kannada   Brahmaputra
Rupee   Ganges
New Delhi   Taj Mahal
Calcutta   Kabaddi
Kanchenjunga   Curry

b Check with a classmate. Then tell the class.

66 Kannada is ... 99

c 📼 Listen again. What is India's position in these categories?

largest countries in Asia
largest countries in the world
most populated countries in the world
largest English-speaking countries

8 **a** In pairs, write 'Ten facts about ... (your country)'.

b Check your facts with another pair. Is your information correct?

66 ... is the most important city. 99

66 ... is the second most important city in ... 99

66 We don't agree. We think ... 99

You can record your 'Ten facts' and send it to a penfriend.

9

a Bob, a boy from Jamaica, is visiting Jane's school. Read Jane's questions. Do you know any of the answers?

- Hello. What's your name?

* Bob.

- Where are you from?

* Jamaica.

- Jamaica? Where's that?

* _____

- I don't know anything about Jamaica. What's it famous for?

* _____

- What's the population?

* _____

- What's the capital?

* _____

- What language do people speak in Jamaica?

* _____

- What's the most popular sport?

* _____

- It sounds very interesting. I'd like to go there.

b Listen to Jane and Bob's conversation and check or complete your information.

c Work in groups, and think of more questions you can ask about a country. Tell the class.

10

a Imagine you are from a new country. Make up a name for it, and write information about it on a fact file. Make it sound real.

b Ask two or three classmates for information about 'their' countries.

> "Hello! What's your name?"

> "Where are you from?"

> "How do you spell that?"

c Tell your class about anything funny.

> "Julio's from Tongo, an archipelago in the Mediterranean Sea. They speak Tongolese, Russian and Spanish."

TEN FACTS ABOUT A COUNTRY

STEP 1

Write or record ten facts about any country in the world. Don't give the name of the country in your fact file.
There are about 200 countries in the world, so there are many to choose from!

> **TEN FACTS ABOUT ...**
> This country is ...
> It has ...

Write your name on your fact file or on the cassette. Leave it on your desk.

STEP 2

Read or listen to some of your classmates' fact files. Do you know which countries they are describing? Write down the names.

> Student's name   Name of country
> Julia   Paraguay

Check with your classmates if you're not sure.

❝ Is this country in the west of South America? ❞

STEP 3

Check with the class.

❝ I think Julia's country is Paraguay. ❞

❝ Yes, that's correct. ❞

3 My Town

In this unit you are going to learn to talk about towns and cities.
At the end of the unit you will be able to:
• prepare an information pack about your town
Now study the final task on page 20.

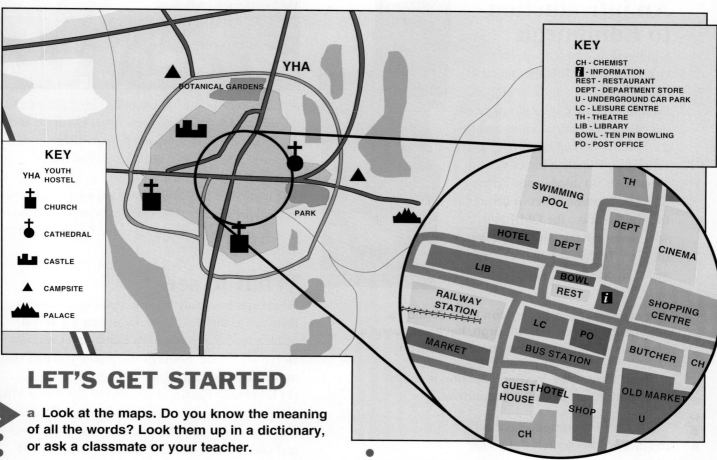

KEY

CH - CHEMIST
i - INFORMATION
REST - RESTAURANT
DEPT - DEPARTMENT STORE
U - UNDERGROUND CAR PARK
LC - LEISURE CENTRE
TH - THEATRE
LIB - LIBRARY
BOWL - TEN PIN BOWLING
PO - POST OFFICE

KEY

YHA — YOUTH HOSTEL
✝ — CHURCH
♦ — CATHEDRAL
🏰 — CASTLE
▲ — CAMPSITE
⛰ — PALACE

LET'S GET STARTED

1

a Look at the maps. Do you know the meaning
of all the words? Look them up in a dictionary,
or ask a classmate or your teacher.

b Write the words in your notebook under the
following headings. Work in pairs and check
with your partner.

Historic monuments	Leisure/sports facilities
Accommodation	Shops and services

“ What have you got under
‘historic monuments’? ”

c Can you add more words to your lists? Tell
your partner.

Help each other learn the new words.
Think of places in your area and then test
each other.

“ Odeon. ”

“ That's a cinema. ”

2

a 📼 Listen to the words in the box. Find their
meaning and find examples on the map.

in front of	behind	under	near
next to	opposite	between	

“ The car park is under the Old Market. ”

EDINBURGH

An introduction to Edinburgh

Edinburgh is one of the loveliest cities in Europe. It is the capital of Scotland and it is in the south, on the east coast. To the south there are the beautiful Pentland Hills, and to the north is Leith, Edinburgh's port. Edinburgh is quite a big city, with about 500,000 inhabitants. Princes Street is the main street. It divides the city into two: the Old Town, with many historic buildings, and the New Town, with its elegant 18th and 19th century buildings. Princes

Street is very beautiful. On one side of the street there is a park called Princes Street Gardens, and opposite the gardens there are many shops and department stores that sell a variety of things.

The castle, the most important landmark, dates back to the 11th century. The Old Town grew up around it, and in 1436 Edinburgh became the capital of Scotland.

What to see

Edinburgh has many historic buildings. Most of them are in the Old Town, in or near the Royal Mile, a road that leads from Edinburgh Castle to Holyrood Palace. Some of the places you can visit in the Royal Mile are:

(1) Edinburgh Castle, at one end of the Royal Mile, on a volcanic rock above Princes Street Gardens. The castle was one of the residences of the kings and queens of Scotland. Now it is a museum of armour and weapons. Outside the castle is the place where they burned witches in the Middle Ages. From the Castle there are good views of the city.

(2) Holyrood Palace, at the other end of the Royal Mile. This is where Queen Elizabeth stays when she visits Edinburgh.

(3) Camera Obscura, at the top of the Royal Mile, next to the castle. It has a giant 19th-century camera that projects live images of the city.

(4) John Knox House, one of the best examples of a medieval house in Scotland. It is a museum about life in Scotland in the 16th century.

(5) The Museum of Childhood, opposite John Knox House. This is a museum of toys, dolls and games from all periods of history.

3 ▶ **The students from Broughton High School, a secondary school in Edinburgh, have sent Jane's class an information pack about Edinburgh.**

a Read the article. In which section is there information on ...? Tell your partner.

> ❝ I think the introduction has information on history. ❞

1 history
2 geographical location
3 shops
4 places of interest
5 restaurants
6 sports facilities
7 cinemas
8 youth hostels

b Read the article again and find the names of ...
1 two streets
2 two places to visit
3 a museum
4 a disco
5 a hotel
6 a restaurant

What to do

There is a lot to do in Edinburgh. If you like the cinema, there is a centre called the UCI, on the outskirts of the city, that has twelve cinemas in one building! There are also lots of discos. One that is very popular is Buster Brown's, in the centre.

Edinburgh has many indoor swimming pools and leisure and sports centres. In the Commonwealth Pool you can have a swim or go down a giant flume, and at Meadowbank Sports Centre you can practise lots of sports, from rock climbing to archery. And in the hills near the city is Hillend Ski Centre. It has a dry ski slope where you can ski throughout the year.

Where to stay

There are lots of hotels in Edinburgh. Some are very expensive, like the Caledonian Hotel, one of the best in the city. For cheaper accommodation, there are two youth hostels where you can stay a few nights, and there are also some guest houses that accept school groups. On the outskirts of the city there are campsites where you can put up your tent or hire a caravan.

Where to eat

Edinburgh has many restaurants, burger bars, pizzerias and fish and chip shops. For something different, you can go to Fat Sam's, a restaurant that serves American food and has live music.

IN YOUR OWN WORDS

In the text you can find useful language for giving information about places.

A *THAT / WHERE*

Find these sentences in the paragraphs on 'What to do' and 'Where to stay'. Join them with *that* or *where*.
1. There is a centre called the UCI.
   It has twelve cinemas in one building.
2. There are some guest houses.
   They accept school groups.
3. It has a dry ski slope.
   You can ski throughout the year.
4. There are two youth hostels.
   You can stay a few nights.

When do you use *that*? When do you use *where*? What happens in your language?

B PREPOSITIONS OF PLACE

in / on / at

Find these phrases in the text. Complete them with *in, on* or *at*.
_____ the centre
_____ the south
_____ the Royal Mile
_____ the hills
_____ the outskirts
_____ the coast
_____ one end

What preposition do you use in your language for each phrase? Do you use one or more than one?

Find phrases with other prepositions of place in the section 'What to see'. Are these prepostions used differently in your language?

4

a Look at the map of the centre of Edinburgh prepared by the students of Broughton High School. Can you find the following places on the map? Work in pairs and tell your partner.

1 It's in Waverley Bridge, next to the shopping centre.
2 It's a theatre in Princes Street Gardens, below the castle.
3 It's behind St James' Shopping Centre.
4 It's opposite the Museum of Childhood.
5 It's in Queen Street, near the Bus Station.

b Choose five places on the map, but don't tell your partner which places they are. Write a sentence describing exactly where each place is. Then read your sentences to your partner. Can your partner work out which places you are describing?

❝It's in Waverley Bridge, next to the Waverley shopping centre.❞

❝The railway station.❞

HOW DO YOU SAY IT?
Sentence Rhythm

a 📼 Listen.Pay attention to the stress.
1 It's next to the railway.
2 It's near the library.
3 It's on the outskirts.

b 📼 Mark the stress. Then listen and check.
1 It's behind the station.
2 It's opposite the hotel.
3 It's outside the cinema.
4 It's on the coast.
5 It's in the south.

c Draw a map of a small town you know, or an imaginary town. Name some of the streets and number some of the buildings. Then write or record some sentences about where the buildings are. Show your partner the map and your sentences. Can your partner work out which places you are describing?

There's a restaurant in_____, opposite____.
The railway station is _____,

Key:
1 Edinburgh Castle
2 National Gallery of Scotland
3 Royal Scottish Academy
4 St Giles' Cathedral
5 Caledonian Hotel
6 Ross Open Air Theatre
7 Waverley Railway Station
8 Waverley Shopping Centre.
9 Main Post Office
10 St James' Shopping Centre
11 Bus Station
12 Tourist Information Office
13 John Knox House
14 Museum of Childhood
15 Holyrood Palace
16 Royal Musuem of Scotland

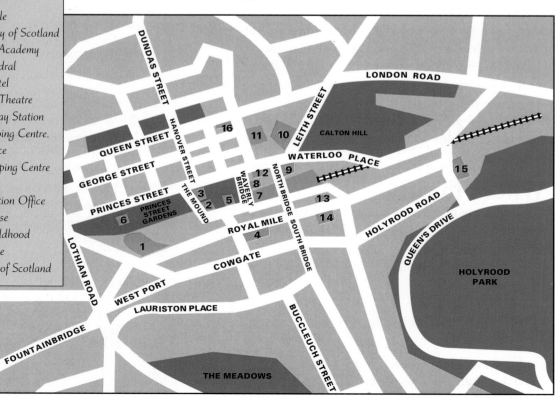

5 Look at the information about places in Edinburgh. The students from Broughton High School have jumbled up the information to make a game.

The Scotch House	museum	you can make your own pizza.
Mr Boni's		has flumes and a wave machine.
	leisure centre	you can do scuba diving.
Mr Mario's		you can have the best
Leith Waterworld	library	ice cream in Edinburgh.
The People's Story		you can play ten pin bowling.
	restaurant	tells the story of ordinary
South Queensferry		Edinburgh people.
Megabowl Park	swimming-pool	you can buy tartan scarves
		and skirts.
Blue Dolphin	shop	has computer games.

a Look carefully at the names of the places. Can you work out what kind of places they are? Match each place with one of the descriptions on the right and make sentences. Then check with a classmate.

> ❝ I think Mr Mario's is a restaurant where you can make your own pizza. ❞

> ❝ I think so too. ❞

> ❝ I don't think so. I think it's a ... ❞

b 🎧 Listen to a student from Edinburgh speaking about these places and check your answers.

6 **a** Think of some places in your town, but don't tell your partner which places they are. Write sentences describing the places and where they are.

b Read your sentences to your partner. Can your partner work out which place you are describing?

> ❝ In _____ Street there is a shop that sells postcards and souvenirs. ❞

> ❝ Is that ...? ❞

THE ROYAL MUSEUM OF SCOTLAND
Chambers Street, Edinburgh
The Royal Museum of Scotland is a great place for Sunday afternoons. It has permanent collections of natural history, science and technology exhibits. It also has an exhibition about life on our planet, with plants and animals from all over the world, computer programmes and an audiovisual show.
Monday-Saturday: 10.00am-5.00pm
Sunday: 12.00pm-5.00pm. Admission free.

THE ROYAL BOTANIC GARDEN
Inverleith Row, Edinburgh
The Royal Botanic Garden is in the centre of Edinburgh, only 15 minutes from Princes Street. It has a collection of beautiful and exotic plants and trees from around the world. It has huge glasshouses where tropical plants and trees grow. The glasshouses are great in winter because it's very warm inside. And in the summer, you can sunbathe outside on the grass.
Open daily 10am-5pm. Admission free.

EDINBURGH BUTTERFLY & INSECT WORLD
On the A7 towards Dalkeith
This is a wonderful place, with lots of tropical plants and hundreds of colorful butterflies flying around an exotic rainforest. There's also an ant colony, tarantulas and scorpions, and a garden exhibit where you can see honey bees making honey. It's very interesting and beautiful. The Edinburgh Butterfly & Insect World is 8 kilometres south of Edinburgh. To get there, take the Number 3 bus.
Open 10am-5.00pm daily (1 March-8 January)

DEEP SEA WORLD
North Queensferry, Fife
Deep Sea World has many sea-life exhibits with exotic fish. There's also an open aquarium where you can touch starfish, lobsters and baby sharks! But the most impressive part is an underwater transparent tunnel. It's the largest in the world and you can see many types of fish, including sharks and giant rays. There is a very good shop where you can buy souvenirs or gifts.
Open all year 10.00-18.00 (Summer: 9.30 - 20.00). Easy access from Edinburgh by car, bus or train. Admission: £4.50 Under 14s £2.50

7 **a** Read about some of the favourite places of the students at Broughton High School. Can you find the names of the following places?
1 Here you can see honey bees making honey.
2 Here you can see exotic plants and trees.
3 This one is closed in winter.
4 Here you can walk under the sea!
5 These two centres are outside Edinburgh.
6 It opens Sunday afternoons.
7 These two places are free.
8 It closes at eight in the summer.
9 This one has a very good shop.
10 It's warm in winter and sunny in summer.

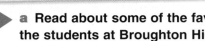

b Which of the four places would you most like to see? Why? Speak to your classmates. Which would they like to see? Is there a favourite in your group?

> 66 I'd like to go to ... because I like ... and ... 99

c Do you have a favourite place near where you live? Write an information card about it. Don't write the name of the place. Then exchange your card with your partner. Does your partner know which place it is?

8 a You're going to listen to two young people talking about where they live: Sydney and San Francisco. What do you know about these places? Tell the class.

> 66 Sydney is in Australia. 99

b 📼 Listen. Is the following information true or false? Check with a classmate.
1a Sydney is the oldest city in New South Wales.
 b It has a population of five million.
 c The Motor Museum has a collection of old cars.
2a Alcatraz Island is a prison.
 b There's an aquarium at Golden Gate Park.
 c The Giants are San Francisco's football team.

Do you want to listen again? You can try and get more information.

9 a Use your research skills: Choose a city or town and find some information about its history and location, places of interest and things to do in it. Write or record any information you find.

b Prepare an activity to check that your partner understands the information. Give the activity to your partner. Check your partner's answers.

10 You are going to play a game called 'Key words'.

a Read all the information on Edinburgh and choose three names you like, for example, The Royal Mile, The Caledonian, Meadowbank.

b Work in pairs. What can your partner tell you about your places?

> 66 Tell me about the Royal Mile. 99

> 66 It's a road in the Old Town. It leads from the Castle to ... 99

> 66 Sorry, I don't remember anything. 99

Is this activity useful? You can read the text again and play 'Key words' with other classmates.

AN INFORMATION PACK ABOUT YOUR TOWN

English is an international language. Prepare an information pack about your town and send it to a school abroad. Ask your teacher for addresses.

STEP 1

Work in groups of 4 to 6 students.
Decide what information you want to include:
Geographical location and history
Sport and leisure facilities
Places of interest and tourist attractions
Accommodation, shopping and restaurants

Divide the work among the members of the group. Decide who is going to do each part.

STEP 2

Work on your own.
Decide how you are going to give the information. You can have things like maps, postcards, photographs, drawings, recordings, video. Use the ideas from the unit.

Prepare the material. Show it to the other members of your group. Listen to their comments and make any changes if necessary.

STEP 3

Work as a class.
Show your material to the class.

STEP 4

Work in your groups.
Write a letter to the school where you're sending the material. Take the pack to the Post Office and send it!

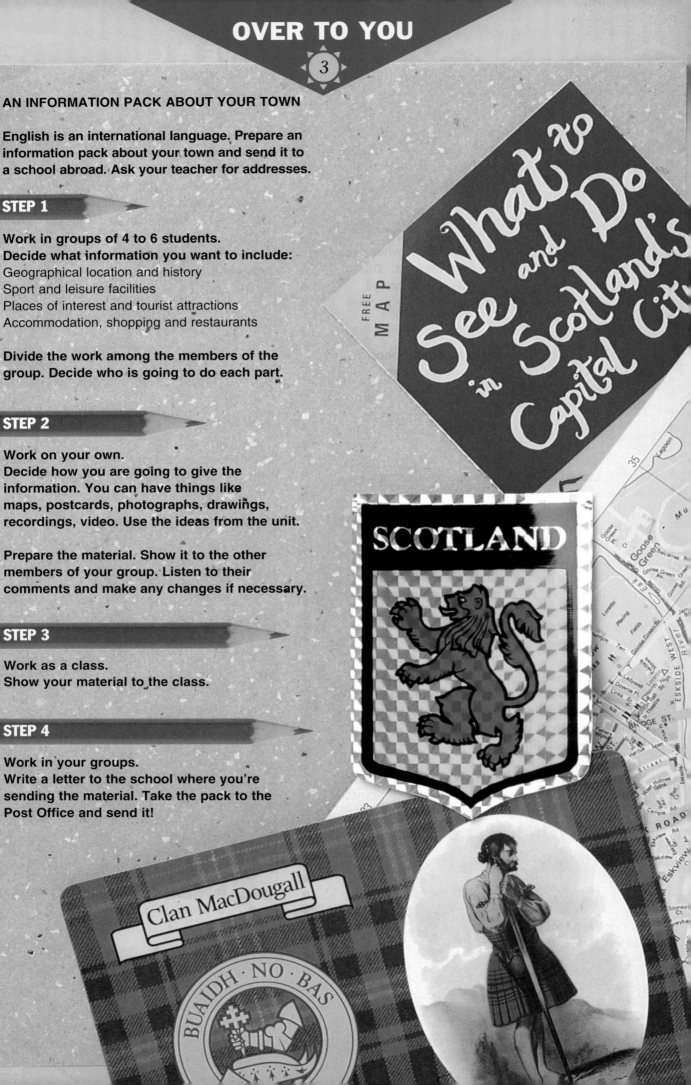

4 Keep Fit

In this unit you are going to practise giving and carrying out instructions. At the end of the unit you will be able to:
- give instructions for an exercise routine
- carry out other people's instructions

Now study the final task on page 28.

LET'S GET STARTED

1 **a** 📟 **Listen to the words in the box. Can you match them with the numbers in the photo? Work in pairs and check with a classmate.**

> arm foot/feet hand head knee leg shoulder waist

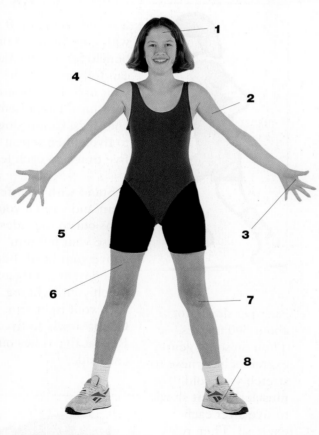

b Check with the class.

> ❝ I think number 1 is head. ❞

c Do you know the words for any other parts of the body? Work in pairs. Look at the photo and test your partner.

> ❝ What do you call this part of the body? ❞

> ❝ The chin. ❞

2 **a** 📟 **Listen to the words in the box. Find out the meaning of these verbs. Ask your teacher or a classmate if necessary.**

 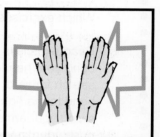
 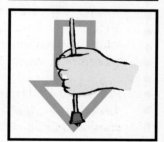

> bend clap count pull push raise drop
> stand stretch step swing touch turn

b Check with the class.

c Which verbs can you use with different parts of the body? Make a list. Then check with your partner.

verb	body
bend	head, knees ...
stretch	arms

3 📟 **Listen to the words in the box. Find out their meaning. Divide the words into pairs of opposites. Check with your partner.**

> above apart backwards down forwards
> right together up below left

> ❝ Backwards, forwards. ❞

4 Read and listen to the article and answer the questions.

a   What is the best way to begin and end a race?
b   In which warming up exercise(s) do you ...?
    stand on one leg
    bend your head
    swing your arms
    bend your waist
    sit on the ground
    touch your feet with your hands

c   Which exercises do you repeat five times?

d   Read exercises 1 - 5 again. How should you ...?
    bend your head   (1)
    stretch forward   (2)
    bend to the right   (3)
    swing your arms   (4)
    push your knees towards the ground   (5)

Tips for improving your running

Warming Up

Careful preparation before a race is important. Warming up prepares your body for exercise. Here are a few simple warm-up exercises for you to try.

First jog slowly for about 800 metres. Then do some gentle exercises like these to stretch your cold muscles. Count slowly to five after each exercise. Then relax and repeat the exercise.

1 Stand with your feet apart. Bend your head slowly to the right. Don't move your shoulders. Then bend your head slowly to the left. Relax your shoulders. Then bend your head forwards. Repeat three times.

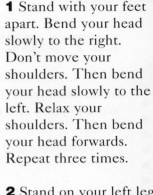

2 Stand on your left leg with your right leg on a bench. Stretch forward carefully and touch your right foot. Bend your hips. Don't bend your legs. Count slowly to five. Then repeat five times on each leg.

3 Stand with your feet apart and stretch your arms out to the sides. Raise your left arm above your head. Bend to the right gently and touch your right leg with your right arm. Count slowly to five. Repeat five times on each side.

5 Sit on the ground with your feet together. Bend your knees and pull your feet towards your body. Then push your knees gently towards the ground. Repeat five times.

Cooling Down

Always remember to cool down at the end of your run. Start cooling down with some easy stretching exercises like those above. Then do some gentle jogging.

4 Stand with your feet apart and your hands on your legs. Swing your right arm forwards above your head and backwards in a big circle. Then repeat with your left arm. Swing your arms quickly. Swing them forwards ten times and then swing them backwards another ten times.

Why don't you try the exercises yourself?

Raise your hands above your head.

IN YOUR OWN WORDS

In the article you can find useful language for giving instructions.

THE IMPERATIVE

a Affirmative

Read the instructions for the exercises again. Find these instructions in the text and complete them.

1 _____ on your left leg.
2 _____ your left arm above your head.
3 _____ your right leg.
4 _____ your feet towards your body.

✏️ What is the form of the imperative? Does the form change if the instructions are for more than one person?

b Negative

Read the instructions again. Find the negative form of these instructions.

1 Move your shoulders.
2 Bend your legs.

✏️ How do you form the negative imperative in English?

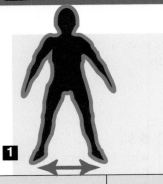

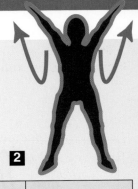

5

a Look at the chart. Find out the meaning and pronunciation of the words you don't know. Choose words from the chart to make instructions for each exercise in the pictures. You don't need to use words from every column.

b 🔊 Listen and check.

1

2

					apart
Stand				foot/feet	together
Turn					
Raise			left	arm(s)	in a circle
Stretch	with	your		shoulder(s)	around
Swing	on		right		up/down
Touch				leg(s)	
Sit					on the ground

6

a Write 5 - 10 different instructions, using the words in the chart.

b Work in pairs. Read your instructions to your partner. Can your partner carry out the exercises correctly? Are your instructions clear?

❝ Swing your arms in a circle. ❞

❝ Is this correct? ❞

❝ No, it's like this. ❞

c Work with a different partner. Give and carry out your instructions.

3

4

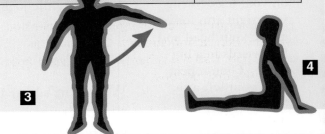

HOW DO YOU SAY IT?

Sentence Rhythm

a 🔊 Listen. Pay attention to the stress in these sentences.

1 Put your hands above your head.
2 Don't bend your knees.
3 Count slowly to five.
4 Step forwards.

b 🔊 Mark the stress. Then listen and check.

1 Raise your neck and head.
2 Don't touch your shoulders.
3 Swing your right arm.
4 Stand with your feet apart.

7

a Prepare about 10 affirmative and negative instructions for your partner.

> Stand up.
> Don't stand with your feet together.
> Raise your left arm.
> Don't drop it.

b Take turns to give and carry out instructions. (Score 1 point for each instruction you carry out correctly.)

❝ Stand up. ❞

❝ Don't stand with your feet together. ❞

8

a Work in groups of 3. Write some more affirmative instructions for exercises on a piece of paper. Use an adverb of manner in each instruction. Then exchange the instructions with another group.

b In your group, pick up a piece of paper and read the instruction silently. Carry out the instruction. Can the other people in your group guess the instruction?

❝ Raise your right arm slowly. ❞

REMEMBER
Adverbs of manner

careful**ly**	quick**ly**
gent**ly**	slow**ly**

9 **a** 🎙 Listen to an aerobics lesson. In which order do the students do the exercises in the photos?

b Look at the instructions. How does the teacher shorten them on the cassette?

c 🎙 Listen and check.

Listen again and follow the whole routine yourself.

❝ Stand with your feet apart. ❞

❝ Raise your right arm right up above your head. ❞

❝ Sit on the floor. ❞

❝ Now raise your right arm slowly! ❞

4

10

a Look at the photos of someone doing an exercise routine. What are the instructions?

b 📼 Listen and check.

c 📼 Listen again. How many times does the girl do the exercise?

Work in groups of three. Use similar instructions to create a short routine for the other students in your group. Take turns to give instructions and carry out the exercises.

> " Stand with your feet apart. Now bend slowly forwards. "

Are there any problems in your routines? Try to solve them on your own. Ask your teacher for help if necessary. Then change groups and try another routine.

PREPARE AN EXERCISE ROUTINE

STEP 1

In class

Work in groups of 2 or 3.
Prepare a 5-minute exercise routine for the rest
of the class. Write the instructions.
Choose music to suit each exercise if you like.

STEP 2

In the playground

Work as a class.
Give the class instructions for your exercise
routine. Use music if you like.

STEP 3

Work as a class. Take a vote.
Which exercise was ...
✳ the easiest to do?
✳ the most difficult?
✳ the most fun?

LANGUAGE REVISION

1

COMPARISON OF ADJECTIVES

Comparative

adjective + -er
short —> shorter
pretty —> prettier

more + adjective
popular —> more popular
beautiful —> more beautiful

Superlative

adjective + -est
short —> the shortest
pretty —> the prettiest

most + adjective
popular —> the most popular
beautiful —> the most beautiful

Look at the two pictures. There are 9 differences between them. Write sentences explaining the differences, and check with a classmate.

❝ In picture A, the man is fatter. ❞

2

a Can you solve these logic problems?

1 John is taller than Jenny, but shorter than Gavin. Alice is shorter than John, but taller than Jenny. Who is taller, Gavin or Jenny? Who is the shortest in the group?

2 Clare thinks French is more difficult than Geography, but easier than Maths. She thinks History is easier than French and more difficult than Geography. Do you think she finds Maths more difficult than History? Which subject does she find the most difficult?

b Write some logic problems of your own and exchange them with your classmates. Can your classmates solve them?

3

Fill in the superlative adjectives to complete these African records. Then check with a classmate.

African records

1 The Nile is the _longest river_.
2 Sudan is the _____.
3 The Seychelles are the _____.
4 Cairo is the _____.
5 Madagascar is the_____.
6 The Sahara is the_____.
7 Kilimanjaro is the_____.
8 The cheetah is the _____.
9 The African elephant is the _____.
10 The giraffe is the _____.

LANGUAGE REVISION 5

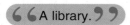

4

THAT AND WHERE

There is a shop **that** sells postcards and souvenirs. Blue Dolphin is a leisure centre **where** you can do scuba diving.

a Find the English word. Tell a classmate.

What do you call a place …
… where you can sit down and eat something?
… that has paintings and other works of art?
… where trains stop?
… that has lots of bedrooms?

b Work in pairs. Prepare 5 similar questions and read them to your partner. Does your partner know the English word for the places that you are describing?

❝ What do you call a place where you can borrow books? ❞

❝ A library. ❞

5

ADVERBS OF MANNER

adjectives + -ly

quick + -ly = quickly
gentle + -y = gently
careful + -ly = carefully

THE IMPERATIVE

Affirmative	**Negative**
Bend your knees.	Don't touch the floor.

Work in pairs.

a Combine instructions and adverbs from this table and dictate them to your partner. Can your partner follow the instructions correctly each time?

Stand up Sit down Open your mouth Close your mouth Say 'Hello' Touch your knee Say 'Bye' Open your mouth Close your mouth	quietly quickly slowly carefully loud(ly) gently

b Create your own list of silly instructions.

Then dictate it to a group of classmates. How many of them can follow the instructions correctly each time?

6

PREPOSITIONS OF PLACE

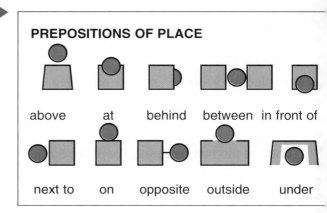

above   at   behind   between   in front of

next to   on   opposite   outside   under

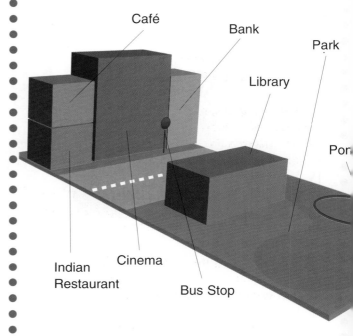

a Look at the map. With a partner, talk about the location of the buildings.

❝ There's an Indian restaurant next to the cinema. ❞

b In your notebook, copy the map without the names of the buildings. Then label the buildings as you like.

c Describe the map to your partner. Then compare your maps.

7

LISTENING

Listening to recordings is very useful, but it can also be very difficult. Compare these two ways of listening to recordings. Which one is better?

Task 1
Work on your own and do the following task, step by step.

a 🔲 Listen to a recording.

b Now write down what the boy likes / doesn't like doing in the English class.

c Ask your teacher for the answers. How many of your answers were correct?

Make a note: ⁴/₇

Task 2
Now do the following task. Read the instructions carefully.

a You are going to listen to another student talking about learning English. Before you listen, make a list of the activities you do in the English class and compare it with a classmate.

b 🔲 Listen. Does the student mention any of the activities on your list? Or talk about any other activities? Add them to your list.

c 🔲 Listen again. Put a tick (✔) next to the activities the student likes, and a cross(✗) next to the activities the student doesn't like.

d Work in pairs and check your answers. Then listen and check.
How many of your answers were correct?
Make a note: ⁵/₆

Which way of listening do you think works best?

Task 3
Read the following list of listening strategies. Match them with the steps in Task 2.
1 Find out what you are going to listen to.
2 Look at the accompanying pictures, if there are any.
3 Try to predict words or expressions connected with the topic.
4 Find out what information you need for the task.
5 Make a note of the answers while listening.
6 Listen to the recording more than once to check.

Understanding recordings is more difficult than understanding people face to face. So listening to recordings is good practice in communicating with people.

8 PRACTISING WITH FRIENDS

Language is communication. It is important to practise with people. If you can't speak to native speakers of English, you can practise your English with your friends.

Making Friends

Try this idea. Do you think it is useful?

Imagine you are in this situation: You are sitting in a café in another country, and next to you is a boy or a girl of your age. You start talking to each other.
You exchange personal information.
You talk about where you come from.
You talk about the town where you live.

a First decide the following:
Do you want to invent a new personality for yourself, or keep your own name, family, etc.?
Which country do you come from? You can use the country you invented in Unit 2, or a real country.
Where do you live in 'your country'? What information can you give your companion about your town?

b Talk to your companion. Try to speak naturally. Record the conversation.

6 6 Hello! My name's... 9 9

9 **a Now listen to your recording and think about these questions.**
Did your conversation sound natural?
Did you communicate well?
Are you happy with your pronunciation?
Did you make any serious mistakes?
Was there anything you didn't know how to say?

b How can you improve your 'conversation'? Talk about it with your partner and make any necessary improvements. Now record the conversation again. Is it better this time?

Play your conversation to your classmates. What do they think of it?

What other conversations can you have with your friends?

10 **Look at the game on page 34.**

Instructions

1 This is a game for three or four players.
The aim of the game is to 'visit' five countries in
the white squares.

2 Start the game from any white square. Throw a
dice, and move according to the numbers you
throw. You can move in any direction.

3 When you land on a white square, answer a
question about that country from each of the
other players. (You have to answer two or three
questions in total.)

❝ What's the capital of ...? ❞

❝ What's the longest river in ...? ❞

If you answer all the questions correctly, write the
name of the country in your 'passport', throw the
dice again and continue your journey.

4 When you land on any other square, answer a
question from one of the other players. The
question can be about:

places in the world:

❝ What is Mount Etna? ❞

places in a town:

❝ What do you call a place where you
can listen to music and dance? ❞

If you answer correctly, throw the dice again. If you
don't answer correctly, stay where you are.

5 The first person with five countries in his/her
passport is the winner.

**Before you play the game, read Units 2
and 3 again and prepare your questions.**

Did you use only English? Did you have any problems? Ask your teacher for help and play another round of the game.

6 Your Stars

In this unit you are going to learn to make predictions about the future. At the end of the unit you will be able to:
- write a horoscope with predictions for next weekend
- read a horoscope and find out what it predicts for you
- report on the predictions after the weekend

Now study the final task on page 42.

a   b   c   d   e   f   g   h

LET'S GET STARTED

1 ▶
a Look at the phrases below. Find out their meaning. Then work with a partner and match the phrases with the pictures above.

be famous   have a long life
fall out with a friend   marry a millionaire
have an accident   travel a lot
have health problems   win the lottery

b Can you think of any other predictions you often find in horoscopes? Make a list with your partner. Then tell the class.

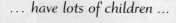

… have lots of children …

c Would you like any of the predictions to come true for you? Which ones wouldn't you like to come true? Write two lists.

I'd like to …

I wouldn't like to …

2 ▶
a 🔊 Listen to the names of the signs of the Zodiac. Match the names with the signs in the photo below.

Aquarius Aries Cancer Capricorn Gemini Leo
Libra Pisces Sagittarius Scorpio Taurus Virgo

b Check with your partner.

❝I think number 1 is Aries.❞

❝What's number 3?❞

c Find out your classmates' dates of birth. Work out their signs of the Zodiac. How many classmates are the same sign as you?

❝When's your birthday?❞

❝May the eighteenth.❞

❝Then you're a Taurus.❞

❝That's right.❞

1 January 20th - February 18th
2 February 19th - March 20th
3 March 21st - April 20th
4 April 21st - May 20th
5 May 21st - June 20th
6 June 21st - July 20th
7 July 21st - August 21st
8 August 22nd - September 22nd
9 September 23rd - October 22nd
10 October 23rd - November 22nd
11 November 23rd - December 21st
12 December 22nd - January 19th

3

a 🔊 Read and listen to the cartoon. Which picture has predictions about ...?
1 health
2 travel
3 money
4 school

b Read the cartoon again and find ...
two good predictions
two bad predictions
two uncertain predictions
a warning

IN YOUR OWN WORDS

In the cartoon you can find examples for making predictions about the future.

A WILL/WON'T/MIGHT/MIGHT NOT

Find these predictions in the cartoon and complete them.

1 You _____ have a long life.
A teacher _____ be very angry with you.
You _____ be poor.
Your friends _____ help you.

2 You _____ have health problems.
You _____ go to America.
It _____ be a man or it _____ be a woman.

✏️ What's the difference between the two types of prediction?

✏️ Now complete the rule: For predictions about things that you think are certain, you use _____ or _____ and the infinitive of the main verb. For predictions about things that you think are possible, but you are not sure of, you use _____ or _____ and the infinitive of the main verb.

B WILL: QUESTIONS AND SHORT ANSWERS

Find the questions and short answers for these statements.
I'll travel.
I'll be rich.

✏️ How do you form questions with *will*? How do you form short answers?

Find more questions with *will* in the cartoon.

4

a Look at the picture of a girl's right hand and read the text on palmistry. What can you predict about her future? Write sentences. Then tell your partner.

> " I think she'll ... "

b Read your partner's right hand. Tell each other about the future.

> " This means you'll get married three times. "

> " And this means you won't ... "

c Are any of the predictions for you and your partner the same? Tell your class.

> " Luisa and I will have four boyfriends. "

> " Javier and I will have long lives. "

HOW DO YOU SAY IT?
Contractions

a 🔊 Listen and repeat.

You'll	You'll have a good week.
She'll	She'll be famous.
We'll	We'll be very happy.
Won't	Monday won't be a good day
Won't	You won't be rich.
Won't	She won't be famous.

b 🔊 Listen again and repeat.

Did you find this activity interesting? You can do it again with other classmates.

PALMISTRY
the future in your hands

1 THE HEART LINE
A long, clear line means you'll be very happy.
Breaks or islands mean you'll fall out with a very good friend.

2 THE HEAD LINE
A double line at the end means you might become a famous writer.
Small crosses mean you might have an accident.
(Only one line for Heart and Head? You might be rich and famous but you won't be happy.)

3 THE LIFE LINE
A long and clear line shows you'll have a long life and good health.
A double line at the end means you'll travel, and might live abroad.

4 THE FATE LINE
A very long line means you'll be a famous artist. Smaller lines across it mean you might have health, family or work problems. An island means you'll have money problems. No Fate line? You might have a happy life but you won't be rich or famous.

5 THE SUN LINE
A short clear line, and you'll do well in your job.
No Sun line? You might be rich but you won't be famous.

6 THE HEALTH LINE
If it starts from the Life line, you will have health problems.
No Health line means you won't have any health problems.

7 THE MARRIAGE LINES
Several short lines show the number of serious boy/girlfriends you'll have. Longer lines show the number of times you'll marry.
No lines? You might get married when you are old, or not at all.

8 THE BRACELETS
Three lines mean you'll have a very long life and you'll be lucky with money. Four lines mean you will live to be a hundred!

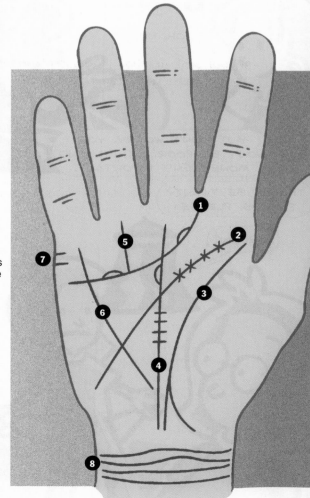

5 **a** Look at the computer questionnaire. Read Craig's questions and look at the computer's answers. What are the computer's predictions for Craig? Tell your partner.

❝ He'll pass his exams. ❞

❝ He might not win the championship. ❞

b Write 5-6 questions on a piece of paper. Make up a name for yourself. Give your questionnaire to your teacher.

Name: Sex: Date of Birth: Time of birth:
Susie Wong *Female*   *July 25th*   *9.23am*
Questions: *Will I ...?*

c Ask your teacher for one of your classmates' questionnaires. Use these symbols to write your prediction for each question.

Yes ✔   No ✘   Might ? ✔   Might not ? ✘

Remember: you can write comments too.

d Find your own questionnaire again and tell your class about any interesting predictions.

❝ I'll be a famous actress. ❞

6 **a** 📼 Look at the pictures and listen to the telephone horoscope predictions for three different signs of the Zodiac. Which sign does each group of pictures represent?

b 📼 Listen again. Write *true* or *false* for the sentences.
1 Libra will have a lot of surprises this week.
2 They'll get extra money.
3 They'll get a letter from a new penfriend.
4 Scorpio will make new friends.
5 They'll get a prize in the lottery.
6 They'll have problems at home.
7 It will be a good week for Capricorn.
8 They might fall out with friends.
9 They'll have an accident.
10 Their lucky day will be Sunday.

Name:	Sex:	Date of birth:	Time of birth:
Craig Duffy	Male	February 2nd	1.50 pm

Your questions: Answers:
Will I pass my exams?   ✔
Will I get a new bike for Christmas?   ✘
Will I get many presents for my birthday?   ✘ (one might be a bike)
Will Manchester United win the football league?   ? ✔
Will I get an invitation to Sheila's party?   ✔
Will I get any pocket money next week?   ✔ (not much)
Will I win the school tennis championship?   ? ✘
Will Mum buy me some new jeans?   ✘
Will I be a famous singer?   ✘
Will my sister lend me some money?   ? ✔

Your lucky number this week will be: ___5___

7

a **Look at these dates of birth. What signs of the Zodiac are Jane and her friends?**
Jane: August 24th
Rick: June 10th
Sally: January 8th
Mark: July 2nd

b **Read their horoscopes from a magazine and find out which of them ...**

... will have a nice weekend.
... might get a present.
... might fall out with a good friend.
... will get some extra money.
... will do well at school.
... won't have a good day on Wednesday.
... will feel very happy this week.
... might have news from a friend.

c **Read your horoscope. Are there any good predictions for you? Tell your partner.**

66 Tuesday will be my lucky day! 99

YOUR STARS THIS WEEK

ARIES (March 21 - April 19)
This won't be a good week for you. You'll have a lot of work and you'll have problems at home and at school. Be nice to your friends, you might need them.

TAURUS (April 20 - May 20)
Monday will be a good day, and you'll be a star at school. The rest of the week won't be very good, and you might have an accident. It won't be serious, but be careful.

GEMINI (May 21 - June 20)
It will be boring during the week, but you'll have a very nice weekend. You'll get some extra money and you'll meet new friends. Don't buy a lottery ticket. You won't win.

CANCER (June 21 - July 22)
You will do very well at school this week; if you have exams, you'll pass them. But you won't be so lucky with friends. You might fall out with a very good friend.

LEO (July 23 - August 22)
Not a bad week. Tuesday will be your lucky day; you'll get a very nice surprise. Be careful later during the week. You might fall out with a very good friend.

VIRGO (August 23 - September 22)
You might have news from a friend from abroad this week. Be careful on Wednesday; it won't be a good day for you. If you are not well, go to the doctor.

LIBRA (September 23 - October 22)
This week you will feel really great. You will be very popular at school. The only problems will be at home. You might have a row with your brother or sister.

SCORPIO (October 23 - November 21)
A fabulous week! Everything will be perfect. You'll have a great time with your friends at the weekend. Be careful with money - you might feel like spending a lot.

SAGITTARIUS (November 22 - December 21)
Don't make any plans this week, they will fail. You won't feel very well either. Be patient. This won't last for ever. You'll be luckier another week.

CAPRICORN (December 22 - January 19)
You'll feel very happy this week and Tuesday will be your lucky day. You'll get something nice: a present, money ...:. Be nice to your friends; they'll need your help.

AQUARIUS (January 20 - February 18)
Nothing special will happen this week. You will be alright at home and at school and you'll have a good time at the weekend. You might go to a party.

PISCES (February 19 - March 20)
This will be a good week to solve problems. Talk to your parents; they'll understand. On Monday or Tuesday you might not feel very well, but you will be alright in a few days.

8 **a** Do horoscope predictions come true? Read these diary entries for Jane and her friends. Which predictions in the magazine came true for them? Which predictions were wrong? Tell your partner.

> ❝Mark's horoscope said he would pass his exams, but he failed his Maths exam. So that prediction was wrong.❞

January 10th-17th
Not a very good week. I did the lottery but didn't win any prizes. Then I lost a £20 note on Wednesday. On Friday I started feeling unwell and spent the whole weekend in bed!
Rick

January 10th-17th
The week at school was OK, but there were some problems - I failed the Maths exam and fell out with Jane. I hope …
Mark

January 10th-17th
A tremendous week. I had a letter from my Spanish penfriend, Saro, on Monday; she's coming to England in the summer. I went out with Libby on Wednesday and had a great time.
Jane

January 10th-17th
A great week. I did a Maths exam on Tuesday and got an A! I had my 15th birthday on Wednesday and got lots of presents from the family. Auntie Anne sent me £25!
Sally

LOOK AND LEARN

The horoscope said: "You **will** pass the exams."
The horoscope said I/he/she **would** pass the exams.

The horoscope said: "You **won't** win."
The horoscope said I/he/she **wouldn't** win.

---

9 **a** Are you a good fortune teller? Work in pairs.

Student A: You are a fortune teller. Think of a system to answer your partner's questions. For example, choosing different pieces of paper or rolling a dice.

will

won't

might/might not

Student B: You want to know what will happen to you after school today. Write down questions you would like to ask a fortune teller.

Will I have pizza for dinner?

Will I meet my girl/boyfriend tonight?

Will my mother give me some money?

Ask your questions, and write down the fortune teller's answers.

Any problems? Ask for help.

b Now change roles. You can also work with different partners.

c Which of your classmates was a good fortune teller? In your next English lesson, compare their predictions with what really happened. Tell the class.

> ❝Luis was very good. He said my girlfriend would phone me. And she phoned me!❞

> ❝Paula wasn't very good. She said I'd have pizza for dinner. But I had fish.❞

OVER TO YOU

6

WRITE A HOROSCOPE FOR NEXT WEEKEND

STEP 1

Work in groups of 3.
Write predictions for next weekend for each sign of the Zodiac. You can write predictions about ...

* health   * family   * free time
* money   * friends   * travel

Make a poster. You can use pictures of the signs of the Zodiac. Put your poster on the classroom wall. Label the poster with your names and the letter of your group.

STEP 2

Work on your own.
Read the predictions for your sign on all the posters. Write notes about all the predictions in your notebook.

STEP 3

Work in your groups.
After the weekend, read your notes about the predictions again. Which predictions came true? Report to your group. Then vote for the group that made the best predictions.

> **"** Group B was very bad. They said I'd win some money. But I didn't win any money. **"**

> **"** I vote for Group B. They said I'd go out on Saturday evening. And I went out on Saturday evening. **"**

STEP 4

Work as a class. Tell the class which group you voted for. Count the votes for each group. Which group got the most votes? Which group made the best predictions?

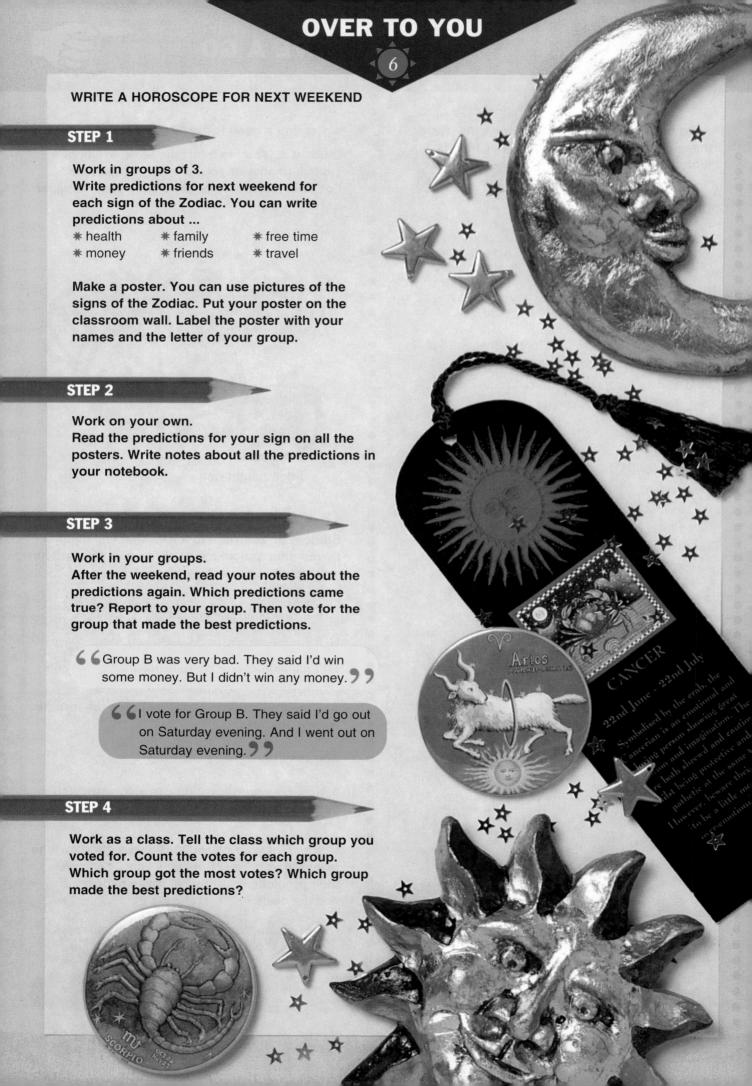

Sports Mad

7

In this unit you are going to practise talking about games:
aims, rules, number of players, etc.
At the end of the unit you will be able to:
- design a new game and explain it to your classmates
- vote for the wackiest and the most practical games, and play them!
Now study the final task on page 52.

LET'S GET STARTED

1

a 🔊 **Listen to the words in the box. Do you know all the games? Look them up in a dictionary or ask your teacher if you don't.**

> badminton baseball basketball football golf
> handball hockey rugby table tennis volleyball

b 🔊 **Listen to the words in the box, and find the objects in the pictures. Do you know what games the objects are used for? Tell a classmate.**

> basket   bat   club   goal   net
> racket   shuttlecock   stick

c Work in pairs. Check with your partner.

> 66 Number 3 is a bat. It's used for playing … 99

> 66 What's number 1? 99

d Can you think of more games and sports equipment? Work in groups and tell the class.

2 🔊 **Look at the pictures and listen to the words. Can you guess their meaning? Check with the class.**

> bounce   head   hit   hold   kick
> pass   punch   score   serve   trip

3 **a** Read the article and look at the photos. Find the names of the games in each photo. Work in pairs and tell your partner.

❝ I think number 1 is … ❞

b Read the article again and find out …

1 where you play each game.

2 *a* how many players there are in a tag rugby team.
  b how you score a try.
  c how you move the ball.

Popular Games at School

You can't play netball? You don't know what tag rugby is? You're joking! Well, here's your chance to find out about three popular games.

Tag rugby is a game for two teams of seven players each. Girls and boys play together on a small rugby pitch.

You wear two pieces of cloth, called 'tags', on a belt. When a member of the opposite team gets one of your tags and holds it, you have to stop running. Then you have to pass the ball to another member of your team.

You can carry the ball in your hands and you can pass it backwards to any member of your team, but you can't pass it forwards.

To score a try (three points) in tag rugby, you have to put the ball on the ground behind a line at one end of the pitch.

The team that scores the most tries is the winner. When both teams score no tries or the same number of tries, the game is a draw.

3 *a* how you win points in badminton.
   b how you win a badminton match.

4 *a* how many players there are in a
    netball team.
   b how you score a goal.
   c how you pass the ball.

You can head the ball.

IN YOUR OWN WORDS

In the article you can find useful language for talking about rules.

A *HAVE TO:* ROUTINE OBLIGATIONS

Find these sentences in the netball rules and complete them.
You _____ shoot the ball into the basket.
The goalkeeper _____ stay near the post.
The other players _____ pass the ball to their goal shooter and goal attack.

Now complete the rule: To talk about the routine actions of a game, you use _____ and the infinitive of the verb. What about in your language? How do you say *you have to* when you are talking about rules?

Find more examples of routine actions in the article.

B *CAN* AND *CAN'T:* ACTIONS WHICH ARE PERMITTED/NOT PERMITTED

Find the information in the article and complete the rules with *can* or *can't*.
In tag rugby: You _____ carry the ball in your hands.
You _____ pass the ball forwards.

In badminton: You _____ touch the shuttlecock with any part of your body.
You _____ only score points when you are serving.

Now complete the rule: To talk about actions which are permitted in a game, you use _____ and the infinitive of the verb. To talk about actions which are *not* permitted, you use _____ and the infinitive of the verb. What about in your language? How do you say *you can/can't* when you are talking about rules?

Find more examples in the article of actions which are permitted/not permitted.

Badminton is a game for two players or for two teams of two players each. You play it indoors on a small court, with rackets and a shuttlecock. A net in the middle of the court divides it into two halves. (The net is at a height of 1.52 m.)

In badminton you have to hit the shuttlecock over the net into your opponent's area.

You have to hit the shuttlecock with the racket. You can't touch the shuttlecock or the net with any part of your body.

You can only score points when you are serving. You win a point when your opponent can't return the shuttlecock or hits it outside the court area. When you get 15 points, you win a game, and the first player to win two games, wins the match.

Netball is a girls' game for two teams of seven players each. You can play it indoors or outdoors on a court, with a netball or a football.

The court is divided into three sections. At both ends of the court, inside each shooting circle, there is a goal post with a basket at a height of 3 m.

Only two players, the goal shooter and the goal attack, can score goals, and they can only score goals from inside the shooting circle.

To score a goal, you have to shoot the ball into the basket. The goalkeeper has to stay near the post and try to stop the ball from going into the basket.

The other players have to pass the ball to their goal shooter and goal attack. They can throw it directly or they can bounce it in their direction.

A netball match has three parts of 15 minutes each.

4

a **Look at the words in the chart. Make as many sentences as you can about the rules for the games.**

golf	hit		a racket	into the other team's goal	over a net into the opponent's area
basketball	kick				
hockey	head		a club	into a hole in the ground	over a net into the other team's area
tennis	carry	the ball with	a stick		
football	shoot		your hands	on the ground behind a line	into a basket
rugby	put				
volleyball					

b **Now check with a classmate and tell the class.**

LOOK AND LEARN

In tennis, you have to hit **the ball** with a racket and you have to put **it** over a net into the opponent's area.

HOW DO YOU SAY IT?

Sentence Rhythm

a 🎧 **Listen. Pay attention to the stress.**
1 You have to kick the ball.
2 You have to hit it into a hole.

b 🎧 **Mark the stress in these sentences. Then listen and check.**
1 You have to hit it with a racket.
2 He has to stop the ball.
3 You have to shoot it into the basket.
4 You have to hit it with a club.

5

Are you a good referee? Look at these pictures. Do you know if the players' actions are fouls or not? Why? Tell the class.

❝ I think number 4 is OK because you can kick the ball in rugby. ❞

❝ Number 5 is a foul. You can't kick the ball in hockey. ❞

6

a **Write a paragraph about a game you know. Don't say the name of the game.**

b **Work in pairs. Give your paragraph to your partner. Does your partner know the name of your game?**

7

a 📼 In schools, students play many different games. Listen to three people describing the most popular games in their schools. Match the descriptions with the pictures.

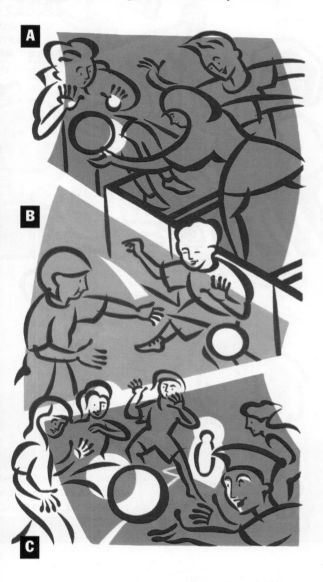

A

B

C

b 📼 Copy the chart into your notebook. Listen again and try to fill in the information. Check with a classmate and complete the chart.

Game	Number of players	Place	Equipment	Rules
Hand hockey				
Chairball				
Skittle ball				

Why don't you try the games? It could be good fun!

8

Invent a new game. This is the equipment you can use: tennis balls and tennis rackets, and two wastepaper baskets. You don't have a net.

a Work in pairs and think of ...
a name for your game
the number of players
where you can play your game
equipment and rules

b Describe your game to your classmates. Make notes of the differences between your game and theirs.

❝ What's your game called? ❞

❝ It's called ... You have to ... ❞

c Tell the class about the differences between your games.

❝ In our game you have to ... and in Lucia and José's game you have to ... ❞

9 📼 **Read or listen to the cartoon. Write *true* or *false* for each sentence.**

1   Foot-tennis is a very old game.
2   There are four players in a foot-tennis team.
3   In foot-tennis players use rackets.
4   You can head the ball in foot-tennis.
5   Angela is in the school's best foot-tennis team.

IN YOUR OWN WORDS

In the cartoon you can find language for asking questions about rules.

HAVE TO AND *CAN*

a Questions

Find the question form of these statements in the cartoon.
You have to hit it with a racket.
You can head the ball.

▶ Complete the rule: In questions with *have to*, you put _____ before the subject.
In questions with *can*, you put _____ before the subject.

b Short answers

Find the short answers to the questions above. Copy them next to the questions.

▶ What is the difference between short answers with *have to* and *can*?

Can you answer these questions now?
Do you have to kick the ball?
Yes, _____.
Can you touch it with your hands?
No, _____.

10 ▶ Work in pairs. Look at these 'wacky' games. In turns, choose one of the games, but don't tell your partner which one it is. Answer your partner's questions. Can your partner guess the game?

❝ Do you have to kick the ball over a net? ❞

❝ Yes, you do. ❞

❝ Your game is foot-tennis. Your turn. ❞

❝ How long is a match in your game? ❞

11 ▶ **a** 📼 Listen to some people playing a guessing game. Can you guess the game or sport?

b Work in groups. Think of a game you know well or a game you have read about in this unit. Answer your classmates' questions. Do they know which game you are thinking of?

Play two rounds. Any problems? Tell your teacher. Then change groups and play the game again.

'WACKY' GAMES

FOOT-TENNIS

CATCHBALL

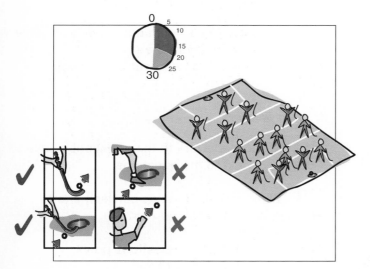

GOLF HOCKEY

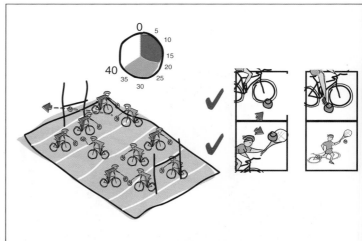

PEDAL POLO

12

a Here are some other less well-known games. What do you know about them? Work with your partner and try to complete the table.

	Number of players	Place	Equipment	Rules
Five-a-side football				
Lacrosse				
Polo				
Shinty				

b Ask your teacher for information about one of the games. Read it and complete the table.

c Ask your classmates questions to get any other information you need.

❝ Do you know anything about lacrosse? ❞

    ❝ No, I'm sorry. ❞

❝ Yes, what do you want to know? ❞

d Check with the class.

❝ Polo is a game for ... You play it with ... ❞

DESIGN YOUR OWN GAME

STEP 1

In groups, design a new game. Think about:
* the number of players
* special equipment you have to have
* the place where you play the game
* the rules

Write the information on a poster.

BALLOON PING-PONG

NUMBER OF PLAYERS: two people or two teams of two players.

EQUIPME... ...cks, ping...ong bats a... ...a balloon.

RULES: 1. You ha...to hit... he ballo... 2. You can ...t touch ...e ba... with your ...nds.

STEP 2

Explain your game to the class.

‎"Balloon ping-pong is a game for two or four players. You need ... You play it indoors."

"In this game you have to ..."

Answer your classmates' questions.

"Can you touch the balloon with your head?"

STEP 3

Take a vote. Which game is the most original, or the wackiest? Which is the most practical?

Why don't you play some of the games during your break? You can organize a league!

8 Famous People

In this unit you are going to find out about famous people from the past and practise asking and answering questions about them.
At the end of the unit you will be able to:

* prepare questions for a quiz about famous people from the past
* answer other people's questions about famous people

Now study the final task on page 60.

LET'S GET STARTED

1

a 🔊 **Listen to the words in the box. Do you know their meaning? Ask your teacher or a classmate if you don't.**

architect	artist	explorer	film star
inventor	sailor	scientist	writer

b Can you match the people in the pictures with their occupations?

c Check with the class.

❝Agatha Christie was a famous writer.❞

❝I think ... was a/an ...❞

2 Do you know what the people in the pictures did? Tell the class. Use the verbs in the box.

act	design	discover	explore
invent	paint	sail	write

❝I think Alexandre Gustave Eiffel designed the Eiffel Tower in Paris.❞

3 What other famous people from the past do you know about? With a partner, write notes about two famous people. Use a dictionary if necessary. Then tell the class.

1 Agatha Christie
2 Vincent Van Gogh
3 Laurel and Hardy
4 Karl Benz
5 Isaac Newton
6 David Livingstone
7 Alexandre Eiffel
8 Ferdinand Magellan

Name	Occupation	Famous for
Juan de la Cierva	engineer	built the first Autogiro.

❝Juan de la Cierva was an engineer. He built the first Autogiro.❞

4 **a** Look at the quiz. Can you answer the questions? Choose *a* or *b*.

How much do you know about famous people?

1 Who was Grandma Moses?
   a a famous artist
   b a famous architect

2 Who discovered radium?
   a Pierre and Marie Curie
   b Alexander Fleming

3 When did Marie Curie win the Nobel Prize for chemistry?
   a In 1903
   b In 1910

4 What did Ladislaö Biró invent?
   a The ballpoint pen
   b The typewriter

5 Was Biró from Italy?
   a Yes, he was.
   b No, he wasn't.

6 Who was the first European on the continent of America?
   a Christopher Columbus
   b King Ferdinand of Spain

7 Did Columbus discover India?
   a Yes, he did.
   b No, he didn't.

8 Which Spanish queen gave Columbus the money for his expedition?
   a Queen Isabella
   b Queen Mercedes

9 Which famous architect designed the Sagrada Familia in Barcelona?
   a Alexandre Gustave Eiffel
   b Antoni Gaudí

10 Where was Gaudí born?
   a In Rome
   b In Reus (Barcelona)

b Read the encyclopaedia entries and check your answers.

MOSES, ANNA MARY

Anna Mary Moses was an American artist. She was born near New York in 1860. She started painting when she was 78 and continued past her 100th birthday. *Grandma Moses*, as people called Anna Mary, painted pictures of country life in a very simple way and won many awards. She died in 1961, aged 101.

SKLODOWSKA, MANYA

Manya Sklodowska was born in Poland in 1867. She went to France to study at the Sorbonne and changed her name to Marie. She married Pierre Curie, a physics professor at the university. Marie and Pierre were both scientists and together they discovered radium. They won the Nobel Prize for physics in 1903. Pierre died in 1906 and Marie took his job at the Sorbonne. She won another Nobel Prize, this time for chemistry, in 1910. Marie Curie died in France in 1934.

BIRÓ, LADISLAÖ

Ladislaö Biró was a famous inventor. He was born in 1900 in Budapest and worked there as an editor. Biró invented the ballpoint pen or biro; it first went on sale in November 1946. Before that people used pens and ink. Biró died in Argentina in 1985.

COLUMBUS, CHRISTOPHER

Christopher Columbus was a sailor and explorer. He was born in Italy in 1441 but he lived in Portugal and changed his name to Cristobal Colón. King Ferdinand and Queen Isabella of Spain gave Columbus money for an expedition to India. But Columbus didn't get to India. On 12th October 1492, he landed on an island in the Caribbean. He called the island *Hispaniola* ('little Spain'). Some people say that Columbus discovered America - he was the first European on the continent of America. He died in 1506.

GAUDÍ, ANTONI

Antoni Gaudí was born in Reus, Catalonia, in 1852. In 1870 he went to Barcelona where he studied architecture. He designed many buildings and a park in Barcelona but his most important work was the church of the Sagrada Familia. He started working on it in 1884 and died in 1926 before he finished his work.

5 **Read the entries again. Write *true* or *false* for these sentences.**

1 Grandma Moses painted simple pictures.
2 She died when she was 78.
3 Marie Curie lived in France.
4 She discovered radium with her father.
5 Biró was born in Hungary.
6 He died in 1900.
7 Columbus got money from the king of Spain.
8 He sailed to Spain in 1492.
9 Antoni Gaudí studied medicine.
10 He designed a park in Barcelona.

IN YOUR OWN WORDS

In the quiz you have examples of questions about famous people from the past.

PAST SIMPLE QUESTIONS

a Subject and Object

Find the questions in the quiz for these answers.

1 _____? Pierre and Marie Curie.
2 _____? Antoni Gaudí.
3 _____? The ballpoint pen.
4 _____? In 1910.

✏️ **What is the difference between questions 1, 2 and 3, 4? Why are they different? What happens in your language?**

Now write these questions in full.
What / Pierre and Marie Curie / discover? (Radium)
What / Gaudí / design? (The Sagrada Familia)
Who / invent / the ballpoint pen? (Ladislaö Biró)
Who / win / Nobel prize for chemistry in 1910? (Marie Curie)

b Questions with *who, which*

Find these questions in the quiz and complete them.

1 _____ discovered radium?
2 _____ Spanish queen gave Columbus the money for his expedition?
3 _____ famous architect designed the Sagrada Familia in Barcelona?

✏️ **When do you use *who*, and when do you use *which*? What happens in your language?**

Now complete these questions with *who, where* or *which*.

In _____ country was Columbus born?
_____ did Biró die?
_____ won the Nobel Prize for chemistry in 1910?
_____ famous scientists won the Nobel Prize for physics in 1903?

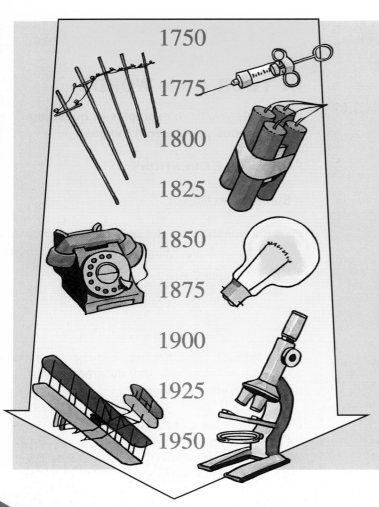

1750
1775
1800
1825
1850
1875
1900
1925
1950

Edward Jenner (1749-1823) *b*. Berkeley, England, doctor; discovered vaccination against smallpox (1796).

Samuel Morse (1791-1872) *b*. Charlestown, USA; invented the telegraph machine (1840).

Alfred B. Nobel (1833 - 1896) *b*. Stockholm, Sweden; chemist and engineer; invented dynamite (1866).

Alexander G. Bell (1847-1922) *b*. Edinburgh, Scotland; inventor; invented the telephone (1876).

Thomas A. Edison (1847-1931) *b*. Milan, USA; inventor; invented the electric light bulb (1897) and the first record player (1877).

Wilbur Wright (1867-1912) *b*. Millville, USA, and Orville Wright (1871-1948) *b*. Dayton, USA, built the first successful aeroplane (1903).

Alexander Fleming (1881-1955) *b*. Lochfield, Scotland; scientist; discovered penicillin (1928).

6

a Read the chart and find the meaning of the words you don't know. Then answer these questions. Check with a classmate.
1 a Who discovered vaccination?
  b When did he discover it?
2 What did Samuel Morse invent?
3 a Who invented dynamite?
  b Where was he born?
4 Who invented the electric light bulb?
5 What nationality were the Wright brothers?
6 When did Alexander Fleming die?

b Write some more questions for your partner about the inventions and scientific discoveries in the chart.

c Work in pairs. Ask and answer your questions.

HOW DO YOU SAY IT?
/d/, /t/, /ɪd/

a 🔊 Listen to the pronunciation of the *-ed* ending in these sentences. Then listen again and repeat.
1 /d/ The Curies discovered radium.
2 /t/ Gaudí worked in Barcelona.
3 /ɪd/ Leonardo da Vinci painted *Mona Lisa*.

b 🔊 Now listen to the pronunciation of these verbs and put them into the categories in the table.

invented cooked designed explored started lived washed died used landed jumped

1 /d/	discovered
2 /t/	worked
3 /ɪd/	painted

c 🔊 Listen and check.

7 **a** Read the quiz. How many questions can you answer in a maximum of ten minutes?

ARTISTS, ARTISTS, ARTISTS
a 10-minute quiz

What do you know about the world of writing and painting? What do you know about the world of film, or the world of music?

Test your skills in this quiz about artists of the past.

Who wrote the 'Moonlight Sonata'?
Who wrote *Don Quixote?*
Who was Emilio Salgari?
What kind of books did Jules Verne write?
Which famous French painter lived and painted in Tahiti?
Where was Pablo Picasso born?
In which country was Bob Marley born?
What kind of music did he play?
Who wrote *Around the World in 80 days*?
Who made the film *Modern Times*?
Why was Bruce Lee famous?
Who designed the Statue of Liberty?
Who wrote *Huckleberry Finn*?
Who was Michelangelo?
In which century did he live?
Which painter cut off his ear?
What nationality was he?
Which famous writer was born in Stratford-upon-Avon?
Which famous composer went deaf?
Who composed 'The Four Seasons'?
Which pop group did John Lennon belong to?
Who were the Marx Brothers?
In what kind of films did John Wayne star?
Who created the famous detective Sherlock Holmes?

b Work with a partner. Check your answers and try to complete the quiz.

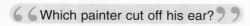

❝ Which painter cut off his ear? ❞

❝ I'm not sure. I think it was ... ❞

8 **a** With your partner, prepare ten questions for a quiz about artists.

b Work with two other pairs of students, and take turns to ask and answer questions. (Score 1 point for every correct answer.) Which pair in your group got the most points?

Read your questions carefully and correct any mistakes in them. Then form new groups with other pairs of students and play the game again.

9 Look at the people in the photos. Jane and two of her schoolmates have chosen them as their favourite people from the past.

Florence Nightingale

Mahatma Gandhi

Pablo Picasso

a Write down what you know about these people. Ask your classmates about them and note down as much information as possible.

> 66 Florence Nightingale was a nurse. She was born in ... 99

> 66 What do you know about Picasso? 99

b 📼 Listen to Jane and her classmates talking about these people. Check your notes and add any new information you hear.

c Check the new information with a partner.

> 66 When was Gandhi born? 99

10 **a** Write a profile about your favourite person from the past. Write as much information as you can. Use an encyclopedia if you have one.

b Work in pairs. Check how much your partner knows about your favourite person. Ask your partner true or false sentences.

> 66 Jules Verne was an explorer. True or false? 99

> 66 False. He was a writer. 99

> 66 Yes, correct. 99

> 66 He was born in ... 99

With your partner, edit the profiles of your favourite people. You can display the profiles on the walls of your classroom.

Time Out

LANGUAGE REVISION

1

> **WILL/WON'T/MIGHT/MIGHT NOT**
>
> I/you/we/they **'ll(will)**   I/you/we/they   **might**
> he/she/it   he/she/it
>
> I/you/we/they **won't**   I/you/we/they   **might not**
> he/she/it   he/she/it
>
> **WILL/WON'T → WOULD/WOULDN'T**
> "You **will** get a present."
>
> My horoscope said I **would** get a present.
>
> "You **won't** pass your test."
> My teacher said I **wouldn't** pass my test.

a Work in pairs. Write six predictions about your partner's evening. Use *will, won't, might* and *might not*. Don't show your predictions to your partner.

Lucia might go to a disco.
She won't do her homework before dinner.

b Show your predictions to your partner in the next lesson. Ask questions and find out if any of your predictions came true. Score points if your predictions were right, and lose points if your predictions were wrong.

Predictions	right	wrong
will/won't	+ 2	- 2
might/might not	+ 1	- 1

❝ Did you go to a disco? ❞

❝ No, I didn't. You said I would go to a disco. That prediction was wrong, so you lose one point. ❞

c Who made the best predictions, you or your partner? Who scored more points?

2

> **HAVE TO/CAN**
>
> Do you **have to** use all the letters?   Yes, you **do**.
>   No, you **don't**.
>
> **Can** you make two-letter words?   Yes, you **can**.
>   No, you **can't**.

a Jane is explaining to Mark and Rick how to play a word game. Read the dialogue and try to complete it.

d	o	t	r	y	e
i	g	o	e	e	s
d	t	e	b	m	s
a	h	e	a	r	e
m	a	t	y	s	a
d	n	y	a	t	d

I'm going to teach you a word game. You see these letters? You have to make words from them.

_____ make two-letter words?

No, _____ . You have to make words with three letters or more. But the letters have to touch. For example, _____ make the words 'the' and 'that' but you can't make the words 'they' or 'them'.

_____ use the letters twice?

Yes, _____ You can use them twice, three times or four times. You can use the letters as often as you like.

_____ use the letters twice in one word?

No, _____ .

_____ use all the letters?

No, _____ . Use as many letters as you need.

_____ make plural nouns?

Yes, you _____ . You have one minute to make as many words as you can. After a minute we'll work out your scores. You score points for a word that your partner hasn't got. For example, you score three points for a three-letter word that your partner hasn't got, four points for a four-letter word etc.

OK, let's play then.

b 🎞 Listen and check.

c Work in pairs. Play the word game. Who is the winner, you or your partner?

Work in groups. Make a word game for your friends!

LANGUAGE REVISION ⟳ ⑨

3

PAST SIMPLE TENSE QUESTIONS

John Logie Baird invented **television.**

Who invented television?
What did John Logie Baird invent?

a Work in pairs. What would you like to know about the people and things in the photos? Write a list of questions.

b Can any of your classmates answer your questions? If not, ask your teacher.

❝Who invented the telephone?❞

❝Alexander Bell.❞

❝When did he invent it?❞

❝In 1876.❞

4 ▶ READING

Reading is a good way of practising your English. You can read at home on your own.

1 Below are three ways of selecting a book. Which advice do you think is good? Why? Discuss with a classmate.

A

Read part of a page quickly. Do you understand most of it? Then that book is for you.

B

Read part of a page quickly. Do you understand very little? Then that book is for you.

C

Read the title and part of the text quickly. What is the book about? Do you like that kind of book? Then that book is for you.

2 Below are two ways of reading. Which one seems better, A or B? Why?

A

1 Read the text slowly and stop when you find a word that you don't know.
2 Look up the new word in a dictionary.
3 Read the text again and find the most important information.

B

1 Read the text carefully and find the most important information.
2 Don't stop to look up new words - try to guess the meaning of words you don't know and that you think are important.
3 When you finish, check the meaning of the words you guessed.

3 Read this extract from a reader. Work with a partner.

a Read the extract quickly. Is the story a detective story, a romance, an adventure, or science-fiction? Tell your partner. Would you like to read this kind of book?

b Read the extract more carefully now. Note down what you think is the main information. Look for information about the characters, the place and the plot. Check with another pair.

c Look at the words you noted down. Are there any words that you are not sure of? Can you guess their meaning? How? Tell your partner.

d How can you check that you guessed the meaning of the new words correctly? Are there any other new words in the text that you would like to know the meaning of? Why? What can you do to find their meaning?

The necklace was in a box on a table.

"Go round to the front of the house," said Holt. "Perhaps Ho is going back to his car."

Chan went round the house.

After a short time the Mandarin came back into the room. Holt was by the table with the necklace in his hand.

"Give me that necklace!" said the Mandarin.

"No," said Holt. "I'm taking it back." He put the necklace in its box.

"Ah Fong! Su Wing!" said the Mandarin.

The two men came into the room. Holt backed away but they came after him. The fight was short. One man had Holt's arms and one had his legs. Then he was on the floor with the two men on top of him. Ah Fong had a knife in his hand.

The Mandarin said something to Ah Fong in Chinese. Then he went out of the room with the necklace in its box.

"Goodbye, Inspector," said Ah Fong. "Now you are going to die!"

The knife was under Holt's nose.

Then a small man came into the room very fast. It was Chan. He put an arm round Ah Fong. The knife went up in the air. Ah Fong went up after it, and his feet went over his head. He landed on the floor on his back.

Su Wing jumped to his feet but Chan was ready for him. Su Wing went over Chan's head and he landed on his back too.

13

5 ▶ WRITING: A WALL MAGAZINE

You have to write an article for your class 'wall magazine'. You can choose from one of the following topics: 'Someone I admire from the past' or 'My last summer holidays'.

How can you complete this task successfully? Follow these instructions. This is what good writers do:

1 GET IDEAS. If your topic is 'Someone I admire from the past', you can write a list of the names of famous people from the past, and make notes about them. You can write these notes in English, or in your language, if you like. Of course, you can look up more information in reference books.

a Read these notes. Can you add anything to them? Tell the class.

b Now write everything you remember about your last summer holidays. What things can you make notes about? Discuss with a classmate.

❝You can say where you went.❞

Write some of your notes in your own language and then look up the translations of words you don't know in a dictionary.

2 PLAN. Plan the structure for your article.

a Look at these ideas for paragraphs for an article about Marco Polo. Choose the best order for the information. Tell your partner.
Stay in China
First years
Prison and death
Journey to China
Return to Venice

b How can you organise your article about your last summer holidays? Discuss with your partner and tell the class.

❝You can begin with the journey.❞

3 WRITE. Write the first draft. Then read it carefully. Is it clear enough? Is all the important information included?

a Read this first draft of an article about Marco Polo. What is wrong with it? What information is missing?

Marco Polo was born in 1254. His father was a merchant. He travelled to Persia. On one of his journeys he met Khublai Kan. He was the first European to visit his palace.

When he was young, he accompanied his father and his uncle on a journey to China. They sailed to Palestine and then continued to China overland. The journey was very long, difficult and dangerous.

b Now write the first draft for 'My last summer holidays'. Then exchange it with your partner. Does your partner think your article is clear, and that there is no missing information?

c Write the final version.

4 EDIT. Edit your work. Read your article carefully and look for mistakes in grammar, spelling and punctuation. Correct your mistakes.

a Find the mistakes in this paragraph and correct them. Check with your partner.

Marco Polo born in Venice on 1254. His father was merchant. He sailed to asia to buy silk and jewels and he sold them in Venice. Marco want to go with him, but he were very young and stayed at home with her mather.

b Work in pairs. Edit your text with your partner. Then copy it on to a clean piece of paper and display it on your classroom wall. You can use photos or pictures to illustrate your article.

5 Read your class 'wall magazine'. Find out if anyone …

… went abroad for their summer holidays.
… went to the seaside.
… stayed in a hotel.
… travelled by train.
… slept in a tent.
… made new friends.
… practised any sport.
… didn't go on holiday.

6 PEOPLE IN HISTORY

Work in pairs. Before you play the game on page 66, prepare questions about famous people in history. Read Unit 8 again and do some research at home.

Instructions:

1 This is a game for two teams. Work with another pair of students. Each pair has two counters. The aim of the game is to choose a colour and move your counters clockwise around the board, starting and ending on the same squares.

2 Put your counters on two different coloured START/FINISH squares.

3 In your pairs, take turns to ask and answer questions about famous people in the past. Before you ask a question, first try to predict whether the other pair of students can answer the question.

❝ You'll know this one - it's easy. ❞

❝ This is difficult - you won't know this answer. ❞

❝ You might get this right. ❞

❝ You might not know the answer to this. ❞

4 Answer the other pair's question. For every correct answer, move one of your counters forward two squares. If your answer is wrong, you can't move the counter.

5 The first pair of students to get their counters back to their coloured squares is the winner!

10 School Rules

In this unit you are going to talk about school rules.
At the end of the unit you will be able to:
- write some rules for your school
- talk with the class and agree on ten rules for teachers and ten rules for students

Now study the final task on page 74.

LET'S GET STARTED

1

a 🔊 Listen to the phrases in the box. Find out the meaning of the phrases you don't know.

> be quiet   run   smoke   touch   drop litter
> stand in a queue   speak English   switch off
> wear goggles   bring food or drinks

b Look at the signs. Match them with the phrases in the box and write two lists.

Do	Don't
1 Be quiet	3 Don't run

c Check with a classmate.

> 66 Sign 1 is 'Be quiet'. 99

d Do you remember the names of the rooms in a school? Work in pairs. Where might you see these signs? Tell your partner.

> 66 You might see number 1 in the library. 99

2

a 🔊 Do students keep these rules? Listen to five students talking about some of the rules. Copy the table and tick *Yes, No* or *Sometimes*.

	Yes	No	Sometimes
1			
2			
3			
4			
5			

b What about you? Tell the class.

> 66 I'm always quiet in the library. 99

TAKE A LOOK

3 ▶ Read and listen to the cartoon. Write *true* or *false* for these sentences.
1 Cindy is going swimming.
2 She goes swimming every day.
3 Angela is a good swimmer.
4 The club has got its own rules about eating and drinking.
5 Angela likes fizzy drinks.
6 Angela decides to join the swimming club.

68

You must eat three meals a day.

THE SECOND RULE IS THAT YOU MUSTN'T EAT SWEETS. THEY'RE NOT GOOD FOR YOU. YOU MUSTN'T DRINK FIZZY DRINKS.

WHY NOT? WHAT'S WRONG WITH THEM?

THEY'VE GOT A LOT OF SUGAR IN THEM.

I LIKE FIZZY DRINKS. I DON'T THINK I'LL JOIN THE CLUB.

THERE'S MY TEACHER. BYE ANGELA!

WOW! HE'S NICE! I THINK I WILL JOIN AFTER ALL.

IN YOUR OWN WORDS

In the cartoon you can find examples for talking about rules.

MUST/MUSTN'T/DON'T HAVE TO

Find these phrases in the cartoon and write the rules.
1 eat three meals a day
2 eat sweets
3 go every day

✏️ Which rule tells you that it is obligatory to do something? Which rule tells you that it is obligatory not to do something? And which rule tells you that you can choose to do something, but it is not obligatory?

✏️ Which form do you use in each case? What comes after it?

Find more rules of each type in the cartoon.

Find two other ways of talking about rules in the cartoon. Tell your partner.

4 a Look at these signs that some students made for their school. What do the signs mean? Tell a classmate.

> ❝ I think number 1 means that students mustn't eat or drink in the classroom. ❞

3

4

1

2

8

7

5

6

9

10

b Work with a new partner. Say what one of the signs means. Does your partner know which sign it is?

> ❝ It means that students must wear trainers. ❞

> ❝ It's number 6, I think. ❞

5 a Work in pairs. Make some signs for school rules. Include rules for break times, the canteen, the playground, the corridors. You can include rules for teachers too.

b Show your signs to your classmates. Do they know what the signs mean?

HOW DO YOU SAY IT?

Must/mustn't

a 📼 Listen to the pronunciation of *must/mustn't* in these sentences.
1 /mʌs/ You must speak English in class.
2 /mʌst/ You must eat breakfast.
3 /mʌsən/ You mustn't drink in class.
4 /mʌsənt/ You mustn't eat sweets.

b How do you pronounce *must/mustn't* in these sentences?
1 You must wear goggles.
2 You mustn't run.
3 You must be quiet.
4 You must listen.
5 You mustn't write on your desk.

c 📼 Listen and check.

6 a 🔊 Listen to Jane and Carl talking about the rules at their schools. Look at the photos. Which boy is Carl?

b 🔊 Listen again and fill in the table. Copy the table and write Carl or Jane in the correct column next to the rules for their schools.

Rule	can	must	have to	mustn't/can't	don't have to
have lunch in the canteen					
leave the school grounds					
join an after-school club					
wear jewellery					
do sport					

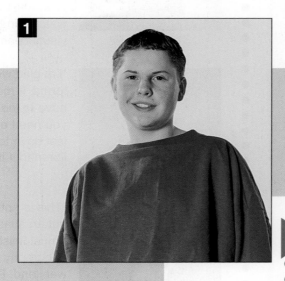

1

2

3

7 a What happens in your school? Do you have similar or different rules? Work in pairs. Compare your school with Jane and Carl's schools.

❝ At Carl's school you don't have to have lunch in the canteen. At our school you must have lunch in the canteen. ❞

b Which school do you prefer – yours, Jane's or Carl's? Tell the class.

❝ I prefer Carl's school, because ... ❞

8 Read the library rules and answer the questions.

1 When is the library open?
2 How many books can you borrow at a time?
3 How long can you keep the books?
4 How can you reserve a book?
5 Can you borrow dictionaries?
6 Can you use the computers during breaks?
7 Can you eat your lunch in the library?
8 Can you listen to language cassettes?

Library rules

1 The library is open for students during break times, lunch time and after school until 6.30 pm. You can't use the library during class times.

2 You don't have to take out books – you can use the library to study or to do your homework. You can use the library during lunch time, but you mustn't bring food or drink inside.

3 Each student has 10 library tickets. You can borrow up to 10 books at a time.

4 You can keep books for 4 weeks.

5 You can reserve a book in advance. You have to fill in a reservation form with the details of the book you want to borrow. The librarian will contact you when the book is available.

6 Dictionaries, atlases and encyclopaedias are for reference only. You can only use them in the library – you can't take them home.

7 There are several computers in the library. You can only use the computers for school work – you mustn't play computer games in the library. You mustn't switch the computers off after use.

8 The library also has an audio-visual centre, with educational videos and language cassettes. You can't borrow these – you can only use the centre when the library is open.

9 You can't bring your own cassettes or videos to the audio-visual centre.

10 You mustn't listen to any of the cassettes on your Walkmans.

Remember: The library is a place for study. You mustn't talk or make a noise.

9 **a** Read some students' opinions of the rules. Which rules are they talking about?

"I think this is a good rule. Sometimes you need to use a computer for important school work, but you can't if someone is playing computer games on it."

"My penfriend gave me a very good English language video, but I can't watch it at home because my family wants to watch TV! Why can't I watch it in the audio-visual centre?"

"I'm glad we've got these forms. It means you don't have to look for the book you need every day. You just have to ask the librarian if it's available."

"This is not fair. I haven't got an atlas at home, and I must finish my geography project this weekend. But I can't take atlases home!"

b What do you think of the library rules at this school? Write your opinions.

I don't like number 10, because sometimes there might not be any cassette-recorders to use.

c Read your classmates' opinions. Tell the class about any interesting opinions.

"Maria doesn't think many people can read 10 books in 4 weeks."

10 a  **You are going to hear three students giving their opinions about three of the rules below. Which rules are they talking about?**

1 Students must wear goggles when working in the CDT classroom.

2 Students must clean the blackboard after their lessons.

3 Students can wear ordinary clothes but they mustn't wear jeans.

4 Students must go outside during breaks.

5 Students don't have to have school lunch but they must have their lunch in the canteen.

6 Students mustn't wear jewellery to school.

7 Students mustn't do the exercises in their textbooks. They must do them in their notebooks.

8 Students mustn't speak to any of their classmates when the teacher is explaining something.

b **Listen again. Are the speakers for or against each rule? Copy and complete the table for each speaker.**

	Rule ... For Against	Rule ... For Against	Rule ... For Against
Speaker 1			
Speaker 2			
Speaker 3			

Why do they think the rules are good or bad? Make a note of their arguments for each of the three rules.

11 a Read the rules again. Which do you think are good? Which do you think are bad? Write arguments to explain your opinion.

b Work with a partner. Find two rules you both think are good and two you both think are bad.

❝ What do you think of rule 3? ❞

❝ I think it's a good rule. I don't like uniforms and ... ❞

c Tell the class.

❝ Pilar and I think that rule 3 is good, because ... ❞

What problems did you have? Discuss with your class, get help and do the activity again with new partners. It's important to solve your problems before the final task.

OVER TO YOU

10

A SET OF RULES FOR STUDENTS AND TEACHERS

How can you make your school a better place for everybody? Here's your chance to draw up a new set of school rules!

STEP 1

Work on your own.
Write two lists of rules, one for students and one for teachers.

Rules for students
Students mustn't be late for class.

Rules for teachers
Teachers mustn't shout at their students.

STEP 2

Work in groups of 4 or 5.
Read out your rules and discuss them with the other students in your group. Keep only the rules that most people agree with.

"I think the first rule is good, but I don't like the second rule, because ..."

"I don't agree! I think the second rule is good, because ..."

STEP 3

Read out your group's rules to the class.
Take a vote. Decide on a maximum of ten rules for students and ten rules for teachers.

Make a poster with your rules and some signs to put up on your classroom wall. Try to keep the rules!

Boys and Girls

In this unit you are going to talk about the similarities and differences between boys and girls.
At the end of the unit, you will be able to:
- express your opinions on the topic
- agree or disagree with your classmates' opinions

Now study the final task on page 82.

LET'S GET STARTED

1 a 📼 **Listen to the words in the box.
Can you match the words with the pictures?
Tell or ask a classmate.**

| airline pilot | bank manager | engineer | soldier |
| hairdresser | lawyer | lorry driver | miner |

❝ I think number 1 is a ... ❞

❝ What's number ...? ❞

**b Are any of these jobs more suitable for women or men? What do you think?
Tell the class.**

❝ I think both men and women can be engineers. ❞

2 a 📼 **Listen to the adjectives. Do you know their meaning? Tell or ask a classmate.**

artistic	disciplined	hard-working	honest
intelligent	mature	neat	noisy	quiet
responsible	serious	strong	well-behaved

b Which of these qualities are necessary for the jobs in the photos? Tell the class.

❝ An airline pilot needs to be serious and responsible. ❞

❝ I think a hairdresser should be artistic. ❞

3 **Read the article. Who agrees with these statements, Jane or Daniel?**

1 Girls are more hard-working than boys. *Jane*
2 Girls aren't more intelligent than boys.
3 Boys are noisier than girls.
4 Boys are more interested in sport than girls.
5 Parents don't treat boys the same as girls.
6 Boys have to do the same jobs in the house as girls.
7 Girls don't have the same job opportunities as boys.

GIRLS
THE SAME O

Are girls winning the war over boys at school and at home?

Exam results show that girls are doing better than boys at school. And many boys now have to help in the house. So to find out about these changes we interviewed Jane and Daniel, two students from King Edward VI School.

Q: Do you think girls and boys are different at school?

Jane: Yes, I do. I think in my class the girls work harder. And they are neater and quieter than the boys.

Daniel: Yes, I agree with Jane. But boys aren't less intelligent than girls, and some boys are just as hard-working as girls. What happens is that they don't like to be the teacher's pet. It's not cool.

Q: In what subjects are girls better than boys?

Jane: I think they are better in most subjects, because they are better-behaved. Boys are very noisy and they don't pay any attention. And they are less mature.

Daniel: I don't agree. OK, maybe girls are better at languages, but boys are better than girls at Science, Computing or Maths. And girls are worse than boys at sport, because they aren't as interested in sport as boys. Boys are stronger than girls, that's why they are better at sport too.

Jane: That's rubbish. Girls are just as good as boys at Maths and Science, and they are very interested in sport.

BOYS
DIFFERENT?

Q: And what about at home? Do you think parents treat girls and boys the same?

Jane: No, they don't. Girls have more duties. Boys don't have to do anything at home. They don't have to help with the housework, or do the shopping, for example.

Daniel: I disagree. Nowadays boys have the same jobs in the home as girls. At home my sister and I both have to wash up everyday and tidy our rooms. And I have to make my bed.

Jane: I think you're an exception. My brother doesn't have to do any of those things.

Q: And do you think that girls and boys have the same career opportunities when they leave school?

Jane: Well, girls can go to university and they can do the same jobs as boys, but it's more difficult for a woman to get a good job. If she has a family, she has to do her job and all the work at home.

Daniel: I disagree again. At home, my mum and my dad share the housework. And my dad has to do the shopping every Saturday.

IN YOUR OWN WORDS

In the article you can find useful language for talking about similarities and differences between girls and boys.

MAKING COMPARISONS

Find these comparisons in the article and complete them.
Some boys are _____ girls. (hard-working)
Girls aren't _____ boys. (interested in sport)
Girls are _____ boys at Maths and Science. (good)

Complete the rule: To say that someone or something is or isn't the same, you use _____ + adjective + _____.
How do you this in your language?

Find these comparisons in the article and complete them.
Boys aren't _____ than girls. (intelligent)
Boys are _____ (mature)

Complete the rule: To say that someone or something is or isn't inferior, you use _____ + adjective.
How do you do this in your language?

Find these comparisons in the article and write them in full.
boys/girls (good at Science)
girls/boys (bad at sport)

What is the comparative form of *good* and *bad* ?

Do you remember how to say that someone or something is superior? Tell your partner and find examples in the article.

4 What do you think? Use the adjectives in the box to make sentences comparing boys and girls.

artistic	hard-working	honest	intelligent
mature	noisy	quiet	responsible
serious	strong	well-behaved	

Girls are more hard-working than boys.
They are as intelligent as boys.

b Work in pairs. Does your partner agree or disagree with your opinions? Make a note of the things that you agree on.

❝ I think girls are more hard-working than boys. What do you think? ❞

❝ I don't agree. I think boys are as hard-working as girls. ❞

REMEMBER
I agree. I don't agree./I disagree.

c Tell the class about the things you agree on.

❝ Juan and I think that ... ❞

Conduct an opinion poll. What are the results?

HOW DO YOU SAY IT?
Sentence Rhythm

a 🔊 Listen and repeat. Pay attention to the stress.
1 Boys are as intelligent as girls.
2 Boys aren't as neat as girls.
3 Boys are less hard-working than girls.
4 Boys are better than girls at sport.

b Mark the stress in these sentences.
1 Girls are less noisy than boys
2 Boys are as mature as girls.
3 Girls aren't as strong as boys.
4 Girls are better than boys at languages.
5 Girls are worse than boys at Maths.

c 🔊 Listen and check.

5 **a** Read the mini-survey. Tick the things you think you are good at. Be honest!

Are you good at ...?

Sport
☐ football ☐ basketball
☐ running ☐ tennis
☐ swimming ☐ badminton

Subjects
☐ Art ☐ Science
☐ Maths ☐ Languages

Other skills
☐ using a computer ☐ cooking
☐ doing crosswords
☐ playing computer games
☐ playing a musical instrument

b Work in groups. Each student in the group interviews three or four students in the rest of the class. Make a note of their answers. Write if they are boys (B) or girls (G).

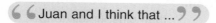

Sport	B	G
football		

❝ Can I ask you some questions? Are you good at ...? ❞

LOOK AND LEARN
good/bad at runn**ing**

c Go back to your groups. Tell your group about the people you interviewed.

❝ I interviewed two girls and a boy. One of the girls is good at ... ❞

d Look at the results of your survey. What conclusions can you draw from them? Tell your class.

❝ We asked ... boys and ... girls. Two girls think they aren't good at playing football. Two boys think they are good at it. So we think boys are better at football than girls ... ❞

6 **a** **Do you help in the home? Copy the table and tick the housework you have to do regularly.**

make the bed
tidy the bedroom
go shopping
wash up
dry up
cook
lay the table
clean the car
do the washing
do the ironing
look after younger brothers or sisters

b **Work in groups. Tell your group about your duties at home. Who has the most duties? Is it a boy or a girl?**

❝ What do you have to do? ❞

❝ I have to lay the table, but I don't have to cook. ❞

7 **a** **Read this student's comparison between herself and Cindy Crawford. Which of the two would you prefer to be? Tell a classmate.**

Cindy Crawford is older than me, but I am more beautiful. I am more intelligent than her, but she has got more money. She is more famous than me, but I've got more friends than her. She doesn't have to do any housework, but I have to. She has got nicer clothes than me, but she has less freedom.

b **Choose two people from the list and write a paragraph comparing them.**
your best friend
your English teacher
another teacher at your school
your favourite pop, film or sports star
your brother or sister
your mother or father
yourself

c **Exchange paragraphs with other classmates. Tell the class about anything funny you read.**

❝ Angela thinks she speaks English better than Kevin Costner! ❞

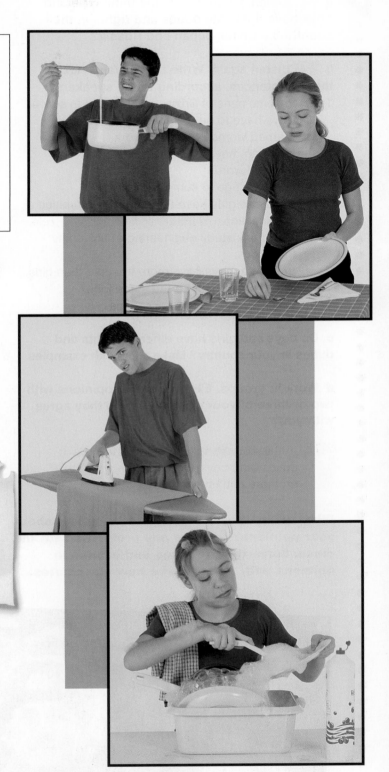

LOOK AND LEARN			
more	money		**him**
less	freedom	**than**	**her**
more	duties		**me**
fewer	responsibilities		

8 **a** 🔲 **Listen. Do these people think girls and boys have the same duties and rights in their countries – China, Japan and Russia?**

b 🔲 **Listen again. Write *true* or *false* next to these sentences, according to the speakers.**

1 *a* In some parts of China, only boys go to school.
  b Boys have to help in the house in China.
  c Married women go out to work.

2 *a* In Japan, boys and girls have to use different words.
  b Girls can't go to sumo combats.
  c Boys and girls have the same opportunities in education.
  d More girls study engineering at university than boys.

3 *a* In Russia, boys have more freedom than girls.
  b Women and men do the same jobs.
  c Girls have to do military service.

c Do boys and girls have different rights and duties in your country? Make a list with examples.

d Work in groups. Exchange your opinions with two or three of your classmates. Do they agree with you?

> " In this country, I think girls have more duties than boys. For example, my brothers don't have to ... "

What difficulties did you have in talking about your opinions? Discuss any problems with the class. Solve the problems and exchange opinions with two or three new classmates.

HAVE A GO

a 📼 **Read and listen to the following opinions. Which speakers think boys and girls can do the same jobs?**

Shelley:

"I think women can do the same jobs as men. We are as intelligent and responsible as men. Some countries have women Prime Ministers. And they do their job better than men. Look at our country. The Prime Minister is a man and everything is in a mess."

Rosie:

"I think women are silly to want the same jobs as men. We're as intelligent and hard-working as men, but we're not as strong or aggressive. So we can't be miners or soldiers, for example. And most women don't like war."

Mark:

" I think men and women should do any job they like. I'd like to be a hairdresser, but my parents think it's not a man's job. But all the best hairdressers are men."

Rick:

"Women are better than men at doing housework and looking after children, so I think women should be housewives. If your husband earns enough money, you don't have to go out to work."

Daniel:

"Women can do any job men can do. Women make excellent bank managers or lawyers, because they're much more honest than men. That's why there are fewer women than men in prisons around the world."

b Read the opinions again. Write a list of the arguments for and against men and women having the same jobs.

For:	Against:
	Men are stronger and for some jobs you need to be strong.

c Which opinions do you agree or disagree with? What's your opinion? Talk to your classmates. Make a note of the best arguments you hear.

❝I think that's an excellent argument.❞

❝I don't think that's a very good argument, because ...❞

Are you ready for the final task? Or do you need more preparation? Discuss it with the class.

A CLASS DEBATE

STEP 1

Work on your own.
What's your opinion? Do you think girls and boys are the same or different? Prepare one or more arguments to support your opinion.

STEP 2

Ask other people about their opinions.
Find three or four students with the same opinion as you and form a group.

Discuss your arguments with the other students in your group. Choose the arguments you think are the best.

❝Your argument is very good, Maite.❞

STEP 3

Work as a class.
Tell the class about your opinions. You can give one argument each.

Respond to your classmates' objections.

Make a note of the other groups' best arguments.

STEP 4

Take a vote. Which group presented the strongest argument?

Why don't you write your opinions on a poster and display it in your school?

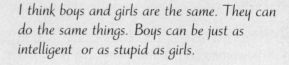

I think boys and girls are the same. They can do the same things. Boys can be just as intelligent or as stupid as girls.

In my class ...

b Speak to your classmates. Find out who has been to the most cities in Britain, visited the most places and seen the most events.

“Where have you been, Jorge?”

“I've been to London, Oxford, Lincoln ... What about you?”

“Which places have you visited?”

“I've visited Big Ben, Lincoln Cathedral ...”

“Which events have you seen?”

“I've seen the Oxford - Cambridge Boat Race ...”

c Tell the class.

“Jorge has been to six cities. He's been to ...”

HOW DO YOU SAY IT?

Sentence Rhythm

a Listen. Pay attention to the stress.

1 I've been to Oxford.
2 He hasn't seen Big Ben.
3 Have you visited the Lake District?

b Mark the stress. Listen and check.

1 Have you been to London?
2 He's visited the Tower of London.
3 I've been to Edinburgh.
4 She hasn't seen Loch Ness.
5 We haven't visited Windsor Castle.

5 a With your class make a list of ...
interesting towns or cities in your area or your country
interesting places to visit
interesting shows or things to see
the nationalities of tourists visiting your area

b Find out if your classmates have done any of these things recently. Ask 5 -10 people.

“Have you been to Salamanca recently?”

“Yes, I have.”

“No, I haven't.”

c Tell the class.

“I asked five people. Three people have been to ... One has been to ...”

Which town/city and place to visit are the most popular with your class?

6 ▶ **a** 🎧 **Read and listen to two tourists' opinions of Britain. Make a note of their positive and negative opinions.**

"I like British people, I think they are very polite. I don't like rude people. What I like best in Britain is the music. I think British pop music is the best in the world. What I don't like is the weather. It's very wet and dark. The weather is much better in Spain."

"I like Britain. I think the countryside is beautiful and there are lots of historic places with beautiful buildings. But I don't like the food much. I prefer Swedish food."

b 🎧 **Listen to two other tourists giving their opinions of Britain. Make a note of their positive and negative opinions.**

c Check your notes with a classmate.

7 ▶ **a What do you think of Britain? Write down your opinions of these things.**

> people   food   weather   landscape   cities

PICCADILLY CIRCUS

b Ask your classmates for their opinions. Find somebody with a positive opinion and somebody with a negative opinion of Britain.

❝ What do you think of British people? ❞

❝ I haven't met many, but I think they are very polite. ❞

8 ▶ **a What do you think of your country? Write a paragraph giving your opinion. Which area do you like best? Why? What do you like best? What don't you like?**

b Exchange opinions with your classmates. Tell the class about anything interesting you hear.

❝ Paula doesn't like ... ❞

HAVE A GO

9 **a** Mark is interviewing someone at the Tourist Information Office in Retford. Read the tourist's answers. Can you write Mark's questions?

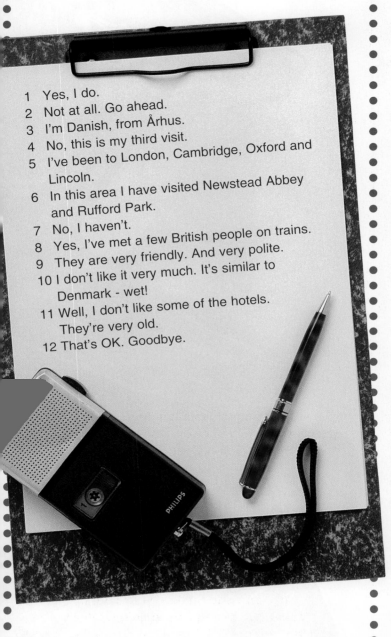

1 Yes, I do.
2 Not at all. Go ahead.
3 I'm Danish, from Århus.
4 No, this is my third visit.
5 I've been to London, Cambridge, Oxford and Lincoln.
6 In this area I have visited Newstead Abbey and Rufford Park.
7 No, I haven't.
8 Yes, I've met a few British people on trains.
9 They are very friendly. And very polite.
10 I don't like it very much. It's similar to Denmark - wet!
11 Well, I don't like some of the hotels. They're very old.
12 That's OK. Goodbye.

b 🔊 Listen and check.

10 Practise interviewing tourists.

a Imagine you are a foreign tourist in your country. Think about ...

your nationality
the towns/cities and places you have visited
things you have seen
your opinion of the country, people, food, weather

b Interview 'tourists'.

Student A: You are doing a project on tourism. Interview two tourists. Make a note of their answers, or record the interviews. Remember to be polite!
Student B: You are a tourist. Answer the interviewer's questions.

> ❝Excuse me. Do you mind answering some questions?❞

c Now change roles.

d Tell the class about anything funny or interesting you heard.

> ❝Marisa is Russian. She has been to ...❞

> ❝Mario doesn't like the weather in Spain. He thinks it's very dry.❞

Are you happy with your performance as interviewers? Do you think you are ready to interview real tourists or do you need more practice? Discuss with your class.

OVER TO YOU

12

**INTERVIEWING TOURISTS IN
YOUR COUNTRY**

You are going to interview tourists in English
and find out about the places they have visited,
and their opinions of your country.

STEP 1

Work as a class.
Prepare a questionnaire for the interviews.
Decide exactly what questions you want to ask.
You can ask about:

* personal information (name, nationality …)

* experiences in your country (places visited)

* opinions about your country
  (people, weather, food)

STEP 2

Work in pairs and carry out one or more
interviews. Note down the answers on
your questionnaire or record the interview
on cassette.

Remember to be polite!

STEP 3

Work in groups of 6.
Exchange your results with the rest of your
group, or listen to their interviews and make
notes. Then write a summary of your group's
results. Make a poster to display your results on
the classroom wall.

STEP 4

Work as a class.
Read other groups' posters and find out what
tourists think of your country:

What are the most/least popular places to visit in
your area, or in your country?
What do tourists think of your country, the people,
weather and food?

Time Out

LANGUAGE REVISION

1

HAVE TO/DON'T HAVE TO

Affirmative

| I/You/We/They | **have to** | go shopping. |
| He/She/It | **has to** | go shopping. |

Negative

| I/You/We/They | **don't have to** | go shopping. |
| He/She/It | **doesn't have to** | go shopping. |

Questions

| **Do** I/you/we/they | **have to** | go shopping? |
| **Does** he/she/it | **have to** | go shopping? |

Short answers

Yes, I/you/we/they **do**.
No, I/you/we/they **don't**.
Yes, he/she/it **does**.
No, he/she/it **doesn't**.

a **Which of these things do you have to do at home? Write sentences.**

do the shopping
tidy my bedroom
help with the cooking

make my bed
wash the dishes
iron my own clothes

I have to tidy my room.
I don't have to ...

b **Work in pairs. Find out if your partner has to do these things.**

"Do you have to ...?"

"Yes, I do./No, I don't."

c **Think of two more things to ask your partner about his/her duties at home. Tell the class anything interesting or funny.**

"Luisa doesn't have to do anything at home."

"Miguel has to iron his own clothes."

2

MUST/MUSTN'T

| I/You/We/They/ | **must** | run. |
| He/She/It | **mustn't** | drink. |

a **Work in pairs. Look at the signs. What do they mean? Tell your partner.**

"Sign 1 means you mustn't feed the animals."

PLEASE DO NOT FEED THE ANIMALS
1

2

NO BALL GAMES
3

4

PLEASE CLOSE THE GATE
5

6

b **Write a rule for each of these places.**

| library | classroom | bus | beach |
| canteen | swimming pool | park | gym |

You mustn't make a noise.
You must wear a swimming cap.

c **Work in pairs. Exchange your rules with your partner. Can your partner guess which place the rule is for?**

"I think this rule is for the library."

"Yes, you're right."

3

MAKING COMPARISONS

Adjectives

as/not as	noisy	as
	intelligent	
(not) less	noisy	than
	intelligent	

Nouns

| more/less | money | than |
| more/fewer | duties | than |

a Look at the questionnaires completed by two students, Enrique and José. Then write six sentences comparing the two students.

Enrique	1	2	3	4
	not very			very
How strong are you?			✓	
How noisy are you?		✓		
How serious are you?	✓			
How mature are you?		✓		
How hard-working are you?				✓
How responsible are you?			✓	

José	1	2	3	4
	not very			very
How strong are you?	✓			
How noisy are you?				✓
How serious are you?	✓			
How mature are you?			✓	
How hard-working are you?	✓			
How responsible are you?				✓

José is not as strong as Enrique.

b Now copy and complete the questionnaire for yourself. Work in pairs and compare your answers with your partner's. Write sentences comparing you and your partner.

4

PRESENT PERFECT

Affirmative
I/you/we/they **have('ve) seen** ...
he/she/it **has('s) seen** ...

Negative
I/you/we/they **have not (haven't) seen** ...
he/she/it **has not (hasn't) seen** ...

Questions
Have I/you/we/they **seen** ...?
Has he/she/it **seen** ...?

Short Answers
Yes, I/you/we/they **have.**
No, I/you/we/they **haven't.**

Yes, he/she/it **has.**
No, he/she/it **hasn't.**

IRREGULAR PAST PARTICIPLES
seen been met eaten slept

a Read the survey and answer the questions. Make a note of your answers.

HAVE YOU EVER ...?

1 ... seen a ghost? ☐
2 ... met a famous person? ☐
3 ... visited the Canary Islands? ☐
4 ... eaten frogs' legs? ☐
5 ... travelled in a helicopter? ☐
6 ... slept on a boat? ☐
7 ... played ice hockey? ☐
8 ... climbed a mountain? ☐

b Work in groups of 5 or 6. Find out if the other students in your group have done these things.

❝Have you ever seen a ghost?❞

❝No, I haven't.❞

❝Have you ever met a famous person?❞

❝Yes, I have. I met ...❞

c Write a short report and tell the rest of the class your groups' results.

LEARNING TO LEARN (13)

GUESSING THE MEANING OF NEW WORDS

What can you do if you find new and unfamiliar words in your reading texts? How can the following things help you to guess their meaning?
pictures or photos
general knowledge
knowledge of grammar
reading to the end of the paragraph
a dictionary

Talk about your ideas with your classmates and your teacher. Then try the activities below.

5 **Look at the postcard. What is a 'cottage'?**

Monday, May 21st
We're on holiday in Britain for three weeks. We've been to London, Edinburgh and travelled around the north of England. Today we're in Stratford upon Avon. This postcard shows Anne Hathaway's cottage - she was the wife of William Shakespeare. We went there this afternoon. Hope you're having a good summer.
See you soon.
    Love,
    Helen

6
a **How much do you know about Big Ben? Make notes in your own language.**

b **Is there anything you want to know about Big Ben? Write some questions in your own language.**

c **Now read the text about Big Ben. How much of it can you understand? Have your notes helped you? Can you find the answers to your questions?**

Big Ben is the popular name for both the clock above the Houses of Parliament in London and the tower which supports the clock. The name was originally given to the great bell inside the clock. The bell, which weighs about 13.5 tons, was made in 1858 and first chimed in the tower on 31 May 1859. It takes its name from either Sir Benjamin Hall (the commissioner of the works) or from a popular boxer, Benjamin Caunt. Big Ben strikes four times every hour - on the hour and on each quarter. The BBC has broadcast the chimes of Big Ben around the world since 1923.

7
a **Do you know the meaning of these words?**

carnations fortnight reach stubborn tiny yelp

b **Read these paragraphs. Can you guess the meaning of the six words? Use a dictionary to check your guesses.**
1 I gave my mother some carnations for her birthday. They're her favourite flowers.
2 We went to France for a fortnight in August. We drove around for the first week and stayed in a hotel at the seaside for the second.
3 They didn't reach their hotel on Monday. They got there late on Tuesday evening.
4 My brother is very stubborn. He always does what he wants to do and won't listen to other people.
5 I've got a tiny bedroom. It's the smallest room in our flat.
6 The dog yelped. The man weighed 100 kilograms and was standing on its foot.

8 ENGLISH AROUND YOU

a Look at the list of international English words. Are any of these words used in your language?

album bar cinema computer club football hamburger hit hotel jeans sandwich star taxi tennis video

b Work in pairs. What other English words are used in your language? Make a list. Compare your list with other students.
Who has got the most words?

9
Read these foreign newspaper extracts and find the English words. Do you know the meaning of these words?

Le plan <<Atlanta>> du sport américain
RUGBY La Fédération anglaise de rugby propose de déplacer le Tournoi des cinq nations en avril-mai dès la saison 1997 avec un calendrier resserré, les matchs étant programmés pendant plusieurs weekends consécutifs, le samedi ou le dimanche.

14.55	Reselust extra: Hong Kong Bericht von Anhalt
15.30	Kaffeelatsch. Talkshow.
16.00	Herra Lind & Heute. Talkshow.
23.00	Samstag Nacht. Comedyshow.

Chance für Verkaufsprofit im elektrotechnischer Produkte
EXPORT SALES MANAGER

10 Work in pairs. Look at the labels and signs. Find the English words.

11 Have you ever seen any English words in your country? Where? Can you remember what words they were? Tell your partner.

"I've seen English words at the airport."

12

THREE IN A ROW

Instructions

1 Work in groups of 4. Look at the game on page 96. Take turns to play the game in pairs.

When you are not playing the game, you are monitors. You have to check the other players' sentences.

2   The aim of the game is to get three or more squares in a row. You must also stop your opponent getting three squares in a row. When it is your turn, choose a square. Make a sentence with the verb or adjective in the square.

For example:

❝ It's warmer in Egypt than in Alaska. ❞

❝ Girls are as honest as boys. ❞

❝ Have you ever been to Portugal? ❞

warmer	honest
been	

3 If the monitors say your sentence is correct, write your initials in pencil in the square. If your sentence is wrong, it is your opponent's turn to choose a square and make a sentence.

You can make rows like this:

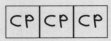

or like this:

but <u>not</u> like this:

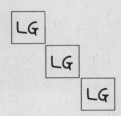

4 Make sentences with all the verbs and adjectives. Then work out your score.

> three squares in a row = 3 points
> four squares in a row = 6 points
> five squares in a row = 9 points
> six squares in a row = 12 points

If a square is in both a horizontal and a vertical row, score double points. The winner is the player with the most points.

5 Change roles and play the game again.

6 Work in pairs and make your own board for the game. Draw a large square and divide it into 36 small squares. Write adjectives and verbs (including past participles) from Units 10 - 12 in the squares. Give your board to another pair of students. Remember to monitor their game.

smoke	warmer	honest	wear	met	French
serious	been	run	delicious	stand	lay
go	Brazilian	play	intelligent	cook	hard-working
better	have	flat	eat	responsible	stayed
be	worse	played	met	Italian	do
spicy	make	visited	interested	bring	mountainous

Break in

In this unit you are going to learn how to talk about actions that were happening at specific times in the past.
At the end of the unit you will be able to:
- prepare an alibi, with two classmates, for certain times during a previous day
- check other people's alibis

Now study the final task on page 104.

LET'S GET STARTED

a Last Saturday Jane recorded all her activities with a new camera. Look at the photos. Can you say where she was in each photo? What time was it? Tell a classmate.

66 At quarter to eleven, Jane was at the library. 99

a

b 📼 Listen to Jane talking to a friend about her photos. Check your answers.

c Which places did you go to last Saturday? Find the words in English and tell the class.

66 I went to the swimming pool and to a party at a friend's. 99

a What can you do at the places in the photos? With a partner, make a list of verbs. Use a dictionary or ask your teacher if necessary.

b

Library: read books, borrow books

b Compare your list with another pair. Explain anything they don't understand.

Find out which verbs in your lists are irregular. Learn the irregular past forms and play 'past tense bingo'.

c

e

d

3 ☐ **Read and listen to the story. Who said the following? Write *Martin*, *Paula* or *the police*.**

1   Last Sunday at 11 am Martin was fishing.
2   At the same time Paula was painting.
3   Martin didn't catch anything.
4   Last Sunday at midday Paula and Martin were in Martin's room.
5   They were listening to a Take That CD.
6   The new CD was Paula's.
7   They had sausages and chips for lunch.
8   They had lunch at Paula's.
9   They had lunch at Martin's.
10 At midday Martin was at the school.

HIGH SCHOOL

Episode 5 **Summary of the previous episode:**
Some pupils broke into Sevenoaks High School on Sunday. They stole exam papers and broke some equipment. Martin and his friend Paula are at the police station, helping the police with their enquiries. The police are questioning Martin.

So you say that yesterday at 11 am you were at Riverhead. What were you doing?
I was fishing.

Were you alone?
No, I was with a friend, Paula Davis.
Was Paula fishing, too?
No, she wasn't. She was painting. She paints very well.

Did you catch anything?
Yes.
Your friend says you didn't catch anything.
Well, maybe. I'm not sure.

Fine, and where were you at midday?
I was at home, in my room with Paula. We were listening to music.

Were you listening to the new Take That CD?

Yes, we were. How did you know?

It doesn't matter. Whose CD was it? Was it yours?

Er ... yes.

Funny, Paula says it was hers.

At what time did you have lunch?

At about one.

Where?

At Paula's. Her parents were away.

What did you have?

Sausages and chips.

Well, Paula also says you had sausages and chips for lunch, but she says you had lunch at *your* house, not at hers. Do you know what I think, Martin? You're lying! At midday yesterday, you weren't listening to music. You were stealing exam papers and breaking some very expensive equipment at your school!

I wasn't at the school and I wasn't stealing or breaking anything!

Fine, OK. Let's start again, if you don't mind. Where were you yesterday at 10 am?

Again?

IN YOUR OWN WORDS

In the story people are talking about what they were doing at specific times in the past.

PAST CONTINUOUS

A Affirmative

Find the information in the story and complete these sentences from Martin's statement.
"Yesterday at 11 am I _____, and Paula _____ .
At midday we _____ to a new CD."

✏️ **Complete the rule: You form the past continuous with the past of _____ and the _____ of the main verb.**

Find more examples of the past continuous in the story.

B Negative

Make these sentences negative. Find them in the story.
At midday yesterday, you were listening to music.
I was breaking something.

✏️ **Complete the rule: You make the negative form of the past continuous with _____ after _____ .**

Now make these sentences negative.
He was fishing.
At 1 o'clock, they were watching TV.

C Questions and short answers

Find the questions and the short answers for these statements in the story.

Statement	Question	Short answer
Paula was fishing.		
You were listening to the new Take That CD.		

✏️ **Complete the rules: For questions in the past continuous, you put _____ before the subject. For short answers, you use personal pronouns and _____ .**

Find more examples of questions and short answers in the story.

Do you remember how to ask questions with the past simple? Tell your partner and find examples in the story.

STEP BY STEP

14

4

a Where were you at the following times last Sunday? What were you doing? Copy the table and fill it in. Use your dictionary if necessary.

9 am	I was at home.	I was sleeping.
11 am	I was in the park.	I can't remember what I was doing.
3 pm		
5 pm		
7 pm		
9 pm		
11 pm		

classmates. Make notes of their answers.

Where were you at 9 am last Sunday?

I was at home.

I can't remember. What about you?

I was at home, too. I was sleeping.

5 Do you remember what Jane was doing at the following times last Saturday? Write as much information as possible and then compare it with a classmate. Who remembers more?

10.45 am 11.30 am 1.00 pm
4.15 pm 7.00 pm

	Jordi	Manu	Carmen
9am 11am	home/sleeping		

REMEMBER
I can't remember. I'm not sure.

c Write a report about the group you interviewed and tell the class.

I spoke to six people. At 9 o'clock last Sunday, five people were at home. Three were sleeping and two were watching television. At …

d Exchange reports with other students. What were the most common activities at each time?

HOW DO YOU SAY IT?
Sentence Rhythm

a Listen to the sentences. **Pay attention to the stress.**
1 I was sleeping.
2 We were fishing.
3 Jane says she was shopping.

b Mark the stress. Listen and check.
1 She was painting.
2 They were dancing.
3 Mark says you were reading.
4 I was studying.
5 She says she was sleeping.
6 They say they were playing.

6

a Look at this 'photo' from a police story. Can you describe what was happening in the park at 6 pm yesterday? Write sentences.
Look up the words you need in a dictionary or ask your teacher.

A man was reading the paper upside down.
Another man was ...

b Make a list of suspicious-looking people. Why do you think they look suspicious?

c Tell the class.

66 I think this woman looks suspicious because she is ... 99

6·00 pm

The helicopter of the Criminal Squad took this 'photo' at 6 pm yesterday. The police think the two people who robbed the Bank of Liverpool on Tuesday met in this park. Look at this photo carefully. Do you recognise anyone? If so, contact the Criminal Squad.

7

a This is part of the report the policeman in the photo wrote when he finished his shift.
Read the report and spot the mistakes.

```
I went into the park at 6 pm.
Everything was OK. Two women were
talking and looking after their
children and another woman was pushing
her baby in a pram. Some rappers were
listening to music and dancing. A boy
was playing with his boat in the pond,
and a girl was flying her aeroplane.
Two men were playing cards under a
tree, and a businessman was speaking
to his office on a mobile phone. An
old man looked suspicious. He was
sitting on a bench with a much younger
girl and ...
```

b Work in pairs. Make notes and compare them with your partner. Then tell the class.

66 He says a girl was flying an aeroplane, but she was flying a kite. 99

8

a Have you got a good visual memory? Close your book and write some true and false sentences about what the people in the park were doing at 6 pm yesterday.

b Work in pairs. Read your sentences to your partner. Does your partner know which are true and which are false?

66 Some children were playing football. 99

66 True. 99

9

a The police found a suitcase with money in it at the house of Jimmy MacTaggart, one of the suspects in the park, and arrested him. Read Jimmy's statement. Who was his alibi?

> On March 26th at 7 pm I was at home, watching television with Patrick, a friend. We were watching a football match between Crystal Palace and Inter Milan. The match was in Italy and Inter won 3-1. The match finished at about 8.15 and then we went out and bought some fish and chips. I paid for them; I don't remember how much they cost. We returned home and had the fish and chips and a cup of tea. Patrick was wearing a white shirt and black trousers, and I was wearing a blue tracksuit and trainers. At about 11 Patrick phoned for a taxi and went home. When he left I went to bed. I don't know anything about the suitcase with money in it; it isn't mine. Maybe it's Patrick's?

b The police want to interview Jimmy's friend Patrick O'Connor to check his alibi. What questions should they ask? Make a list.

> *Where were you at 7 pm?*
> *What time did the match finish?*
> *Who won?*
> *Whose suitcase was it?*

10

a 🔲 Listen to Patrick's interview with the police. Tick the questions in your list that you hear in the interview.

b 🔲 Now listen again and make a note of any of Patrick's answers that are different from Jimmy's.

c Check with your partner and then tell the class.

> ❝ Patrick says they were ... but Jimmy says ... ❞

11

a Look at the language in the box and complete this dialogue in your notebook.

LOOK AND LEARN		
Whose (CD) is this?	It's	mine. yours. his / Mike's. hers / Carol's.

> _____ necklace is this, Mike? Is it _____?

> No, it isn't _____. It's _____.

> That isn't true. It isn't _____. It's _____.

b Work in groups of 4. Draw something (a watch, a CD, money, etc) and put it in a bag. Then take one drawing out of the bag at a time and find the owner.

> ❝ Whose ... is this? Is it yours? ❞

> ❝ I think it's hers/Ana's. ❞

> ❝ Javi says this CD is yours. Is this true? ❞

> ❝ Yes, it is. Thank you. ❞

Do you need more practice? You can play 'Pass the bucket'. Ask your teacher to tell you the rules of the game.

12 ▶ 🔲 **Listen to some people playing 'Call your bluff'.**

a What is José and Lina's bluff?

b 🔲 Listen again. Are José and Lina telling the truth or are they lying? How do you know?

13 ▶ **a** Work with a partner. Make up a story about something special that happened to you last Sunday. Think about all the details. You can choose between meeting a famous person or going somewhere special.

b Prepare questions to find out if other people are lying. You can ask a maximum of ten questions.

c Work with another pair. Question one person from the other pair while your partner questions the other. Tell each other about your experiences and ask and answer questions. You can only say 'I can't remember' once. Make a note of the answers.

> Pere
> went to a pop concert
>
> Merce
> went to ...

d Get together with your partner. Compare your information about the other pair.

> ❝Pere says that he met ...❞

> ❝Merce says that, too.❞

> ❝He says the same.❞

> ❝She says something different.❞

e Are they lying or telling the truth? How do you know? Tell them.

> ❝I think you are lying, Pere, because you say that ... but Merce says that ...❞

What problems did you have? How can you solve them before the final task?

ALIBI

Last Sunday there were a number of incidents in your area. At about 11 am three young people stole some chocolate bars from a shop. Then at about 2 pm three young people took some cans of Coke from a supermarket. And finally, at about 6 pm three young people broke into your school and took some exam papers.

The police think the same people committed these crimes and that they are students in your class.

Help the police by checking whether everybody has an alibi. Your alibi is that at the time of the incidents last Sunday, you were with two of your classmates.

STEP 1

Work in groups of 3.
Prepare an alibi for the police. Don't write anything. Decide where you were at the times of the incidents, what you were doing and as many details as possible. Plan it carefully! You can only answer 'I can't remember' twice.

Give each student in the group a number: Suspect 1, Suspect 2 and Suspect 3.

STEP 2

Work with students from three other groups. All suspects with the same number should work together. In turns, collect information from the suspects in the other groups.

Make a note of their answers.

" Where were you at 11 o'clock, Julio? "

" I was at ... "

" Who was with you? "

" Jaime and Luisa. "

" What were you doing? "

" We were ... "

STEP 3

Work in your group again.
With your two classmates, check the information about the other groups.

" Julio says that at 11 o'clock he was ... with Jaime and Luisa. He says they were playing football. "

" Well, Jaime says that they were playing basketball, so someone's lying. "

Do you think the suspects in any of the three other groups are guilty? Tell your class and ask for a public hearing, if you want to.

STEP 4

Work as a class.
Interview the three suspects in turn. When you are interviewing one of the suspects, send the other two out of the classroom.

If the suspects are guilty, decide on a punishment!

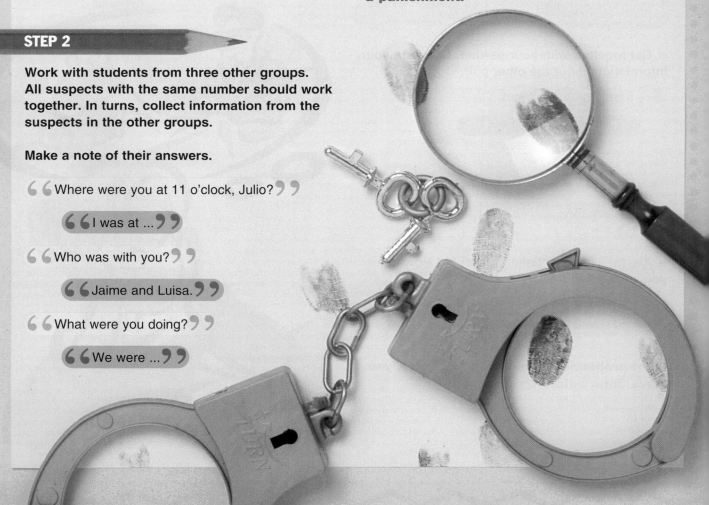

In this unit you are going to practise reading and writing stories.
At the end of the unit you will be able to:
- write or record a modern version of a traditional story
- read or listen to other people's stories and match them with the original
- vote for the most original, the funniest and the best written stories

Now study the final task on page 112.

LET'S GET STARTED

1

a 🔲 Listen to the words in the box. Can you find them in the picture? Check with a classmate.

| dragon fairy flying carpet genie lamp palace prince princess slippers stepmother stepsister wand witch wizard wolf |

💬 Number 1 is a flying carpet. 💬

b What other people or objects do you often find in fairy tales and other traditional stories? Work in pairs and make a list. Use a dictionary if necessary. Then tell the class.

2

🔲 Listen to the adjectives in the box. Find out the meaning of the words you don't know. Which things in the picture can the adjectives describe? Work in pairs and tell your partner.

| bad beautiful clever cruel handsome kind magic nasty old stupid ugly wise wicked |

💬 A magic wand. 💬

💬 A wicked witch. 💬

Find the names of fairy tales and traditional stories in English. Work in pairs and make a list with the words in 1 and 2 that you can use in each story.

3 **a** 📼 Read and listen to this modern version of a traditional story. Find six elements that are not part of the traditional story.

b Think of a title for the modern version.

Once upon a time there was a handsome pop singer. One day he was relaxing in the garden of his mansion. He was listening to his Walkman by his swimming pool when a wicked witch with a magic wand appeared. "I'm going to change you into a frog," the witch told him. "To change back into a person, you must kiss a princess."

Some days later, a beautiful princess was sitting next to a pond when she dropped her car keys into the water. The pond was very deep and the princess started to cry.

Just then a frog climbed out of the water. "Don't cry," he told the princess. "I'll find your car keys. But you must let me kiss you."

"Find my car keys and I'll do as you ask," the princess said.

So the frog jumped into the water and after a short time he came up with the keys. The princess took the keys, ran into her car and drove away without the frog.

That evening, when the princess was watching television with her family, there was a knock at the door. When the princess opened the door, she saw the frog. She closed the door. She returned to the living room and told her father, the king, about the frog.

"You must keep your promise," the king told his daughter. "Tell the frog to come in." So the princess went to the door and opened it. The frog hopped into the room, climbed onto the table and came near the princess's face. The princess closed her eyes and the frog kissed her. When the princess opened her eyes again, a handsome young man was standing next to her.

"I am not a frog," the pop singer said. "A witch changed me into a frog. Please come to my mansion with me. I want to marry you. I'll always love you."

So the pop singer and the princess flew to the pop singer's mansion on the king's aeroplane. They arrived safely and lived happily ever after.

I was listening to my Walkman ...

IN YOUR OWN WORDS

In the story you can find useful language for telling a story.

PAST SIMPLE AND PAST CONTINUOUS

Find the information in the story and complete the sentences.

1 One day the pop singer _____ in the garden of his mansion.
2 He _____ to his Walkman when a wicked witch _____.
3 The princess _____ the keys, _____ into her car and _____ away without the frog.

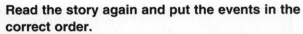 Which sentence refers to actions in progress in the past? What tense do you use?

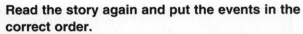 Which sentence refers to an action that happened in the middle of another? What tense do you use?

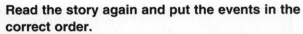 Which sentence refers to actions that happened one after the other? What tense do you use?

With your partner, find more examples of each type of sentence in the story.

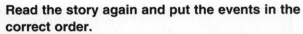 What happens in your language?

Complete these sentences now.

1 The frog _____ (swim) in the pond when the princess _____ (drop) her car keys.
2 When the princess _____ (open) the door, the frog _____ (come) into the room.

Find all the irregular past forms in the story and make a list. Then compare your list with a classmate.

4 **Read the story again and put the events in the correct order.**

a The frog came to the princess's palace.
b The princess lost her car keys.
c The frog kissed the princess.
d The pop singer and the princess flew to the pop singer's mansion.
e The frog found the keys for the princess.
f The princess drove home.
g The witch changed the pop singer into a frog.
h The frog changed back into a young man.

5 **a** Work in pairs. Look at the pictures and write the story. Use the words under the pictures, or look up words in a dictionary if necessary.

b Compare your story with another pair of students.

c Listen and check.

1 Once upon a time _____ king _____ two daughters. _____ Lilywhite and Rosemary.

2 One day, Lilywhite _____ lake when _____ on the sand.

3 _____ alive, so _____ back into the lake.

4 When _____ in the water _____ Lilywhite: " _____ a magic fish. _____ my life. _____ you want."

5 When _____ Lilywhite _____ about the fish.

6 One day, Rosemary _____ when _____ off her horse.

7 _____ very ill, and _____ very sad.

8 So, Lilywhite _____ and _____ the magic fish.

LOOK AND LEARN	
the witch **told** the witch **said to**	the prince ... him ... her ...
"_____," the prince	**said**. **told** him.
"_____,"	**said** the prince.

9 "_____ want?" _____.
  "_____ ill," _____. "_____ your help."

10 "_____ worry," _____." _____ home. _____ well now."

11 _____ happy and _____.

12 Just then, _____. They _____ and _____ happily ever after.

HOW DO YOU SAY IT?

/d/, /t/, /ɪd/

a 🔊 **Listen to the endings of these verbs and repeat.**

1 /d/ appeared	2 /t/ dropped	3 /ɪd/ started

b 🔊 **Listen to the endings of these verbs. Then put them in the correct column - 1, 2 or 3.**

arrived	carried	changed	climbed
closed	decided	finished	hopped
jumped	kissed	lived	married
needed	opened	returned	visited

c 🔊 **Listen and check. Then listen and repeat.**

6 **a** Work in groups of 3 and write a story. Each write the first sentence of a story on a piece of paper.

b Pass your piece of paper to one of the other students in your group. Read the first sentence of the story that you receive. Write the second sentence on a separate line.

c Continue this way until the three stories are complete. Read the completed stories. Which do you think is the best?

Make an ordering activity for another group. First edit all your stories. Then copy and cut up the sentences. Jumble up all the sentences. Can your classmates work out the correct order for all the stories?

LOOK AND LEARN
One day ...   Some days later ...   So ...   Just then ...   When ...

7

a **Read the beginnings of these three traditional stories. Can you match the stories with their English names?**

> Cinderella   Little Red Riding Hood
> Snow White and the Seven Dwarves

1 Once upon a time a young princess lived with her father and mother. She was a beautiful girl with very white skin. One day the Queen died. The King and his daughter were very unhappy. So the King decided to marry again. He needed a wife and his daughter needed a stepmother. But the new Queen was a wicked woman. She didn't like the young princess. Every day the Queen talked to her magic mirror. 'Mirror, mirror, on the wall, who's the fairest of them all?' she asked.

2 Once upon a time a man married for the second time. The man himself had a daughter and his new wife had two daughters. But the two girls didn't like their stepsister. She was very pretty and they were very ugly. The ugly sisters were always mean to their stepsister. She had to stay at home and do all the work while they went to parties. One day the sisters got an invitation to a party at the prince's palace.

3 Once upon a time an old lady lived in a little house in the forest. Every day her granddaughter brought her some food in a basket. One day, as the little girl was walking to her grandmother's house, she saw a brightly coloured flower a little way from the path. She left the path to pick the flower for her grandmother.

b **Can you remember the endings of the stories? Work in groups and discuss the stories. Make notes about the endings. Then tell the class.**

c **Work in pairs. Write the ending of one of the stories. Include some things that are not part of the traditional story.**

d **Read your classmates' stories and find the elements that are not part of the traditional stories. Tell the class.**

> ❝In Sara's story they take Snow White to a hospital.❞

8 **a Read this traditional story. Which of the following stories is it?**

| Aladdin   Jack and the Beanstalk |
| Sleeping Beauty   The Pied Piper |

Hamelin was a wealthy town surrounded by fields of corn. There was one problem - rats, everywhere. The people of Hamelin went to the Mayor of the town to complain. The Mayor said there was nothing he could do. "If you don't sort this out in a week," the crowd shouted, "there will be trouble!" The Mayor put up a poster on the tree in the village square offering a reward of a thousand guilders to anybody who could solve the problem of the rats in the town. The next afternoon someone who called himself the 'Pied Piper' walked into town. He was wearing a multi coloured costume, and carried a flute. As he played his flute, thousands of rats ran out from the houses, following him up the stairs, under the bridges and across the narrow streets. When he came to the river, all the rats dived in and drowned. The people of Hamelin were overjoyed. But when the Pied Piper asked for his money, the Mayor said, "You didn't really remove the rats. We saw them jump into the river by themselves! I'm not going to pay you." The Pied Piper turned around and walked away. The next morning, when everyone was at church, the Pied Piper returned. He began to play his flute again. When the people came out of church, they were shocked to see their children following the Pied Piper up into the mountains outside the town, and disappearing through a little door in the mountain. For years afterwards the people searched and searched for the Pied Piper, but no-one saw him or the children again.

b 🔲 Now listen to the modern version of the story. Look at these words from the modern version. Can you find the matching words in the traditional story? Check with a classmate.

| campers   politician   shopping centre   dollars |
| CD-player   railway station   leisure centre |

c 🔲 Listen again. Can you find any other differences between the traditional and the modern versions? Tell the class.

9 **a 🔲 Listen to a modern fairy story. Which objects below are in the story?**

b 🔲 Listen again. What is special about these objects? Tell a classmate.

10 **a Choose four of the objects above. Write a modern fairy story, and include the four objects in your story.**

b Form groups of 3 or 4 and tell your stories to each other. Can the other students find the four objects in your story?

c Take a vote. Which story is the most original?

What problems did you have with your story-writing? Discuss with the class. How can you solve the problems?

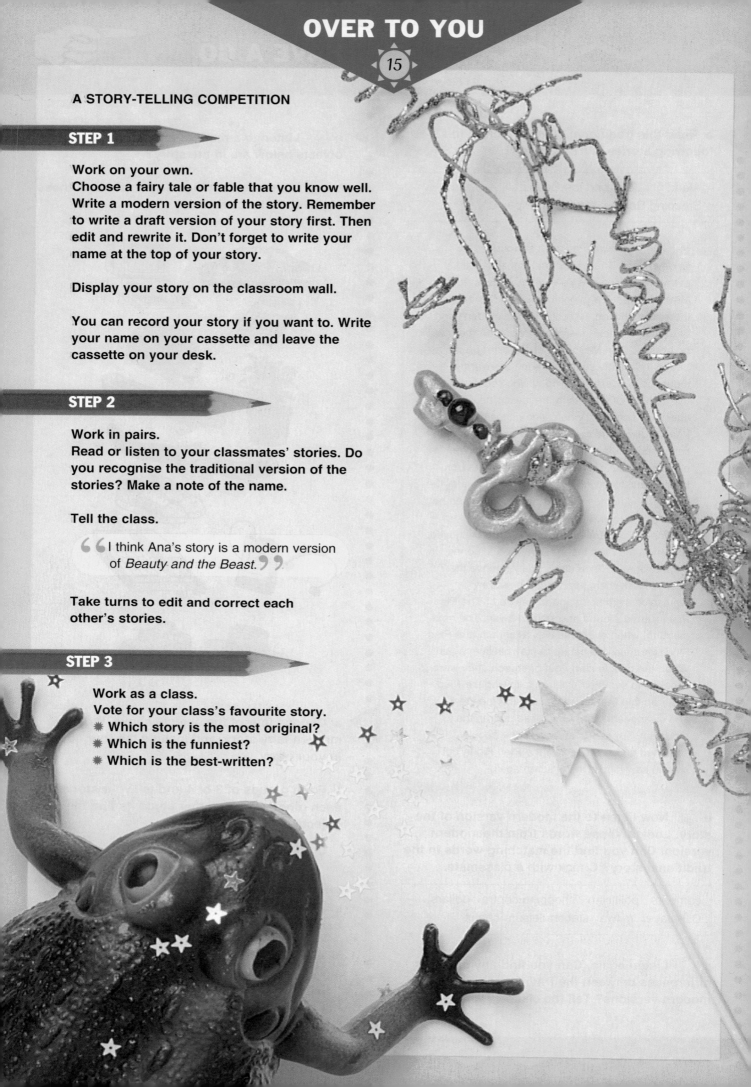

OVER TO YOU

15

A STORY-TELLING COMPETITION

STEP 1

Work on your own.
Choose a fairy tale or fable that you know well.
Write a modern version of the story. Remember
to write a draft version of your story first. Then
edit and rewrite it. Don't forget to write your
name at the top of your story.

Display your story on the classroom wall.

You can record your story if you want to. Write
your name on your cassette and leave the
cassette on your desk.

STEP 2

Work in pairs.
Read or listen to your classmates' stories. Do
you recognise the traditional version of the
stories? Make a note of the name.

Tell the class.

> " I think Ana's story is a modern version
> of *Beauty and the Beast*. "

Take turns to edit and correct each
other's stories.

STEP 3

Work as a class.
Vote for your class's favourite story.
✳ Which story is the most original?
✳ Which is the funniest?
✳ Which is the best-written?

Time Out

LANGUAGE REVISION

PAST CONTINUOUS

Affirmative
I/He/She/It   **was working.**
You/We/They   **were working.**

Questions
Was I/he/she/it **working?**

Were you/we/they **working?**

Negative
I/He/She/It   **was not (wasn't) working.**
You/We/They   **were not (weren't) working.**

Short Answers
Yes, I/he/she/it **was.**
No, I/he/she/it **wasn't.**
Yes, you/we/they **were.**
No, you/we/they **weren't.**

---

a Yesterday at about 9 pm there was a burglary at flat 1A, 12 Baker Street. Look at the picture for 30 seconds. Then tell a classmate what the people were doing at the time of the burglary.

❝ Mr and Mrs Todd were watching TV and ... ❞

b Work with a new partner. Close your books and test each other. Ask what the people were doing at the time of the burglary.

❝ What were Mr and Mrs Carter doing at 9 pm? ❞

❝ Was Jamie sleeping? ❞

a What were you doing last night at 9 pm? Where were you? Who were you with? Ask and tell your classmates.

b Has anyone got the same answers as you? Tell the class.

❝ Last night at 9 pm, Luisa and I were at a friend's house. ❞

3 ▶

PAST CONTINUOUS/PAST SIMPLE

I **was walking** in the garden when I **saw** a frog in a pond.
The frog **was swimming** in the pond.
It **came** out of the water and **jumped** onto a rock.

a Write a story using these words. Use a dictionary if necessary. Can you finish the story?

One day last week/Sue and I/walk in the park/
when/see/boy swimming in the lake./swim/
towards an island in the middle of the lake./
On the shore/a dog/stand/by the boy's clothes./
wait for the boy./When/arrive on the island/
the boy/get out of the water/and/wave to the dog./
The boy/swim back/when suddenly/the dog/
pick up the boy's clothes/and/start to run./
The boy/shout/but/the dog/not turn around ...

b Check with your partner. Do you have the same endings for your stories? Tell the class.

4 ▶

POSSESSIVE PRONOUNS		POSSESSIVE 'S	
It's They're	mine. yours. his. hers. its. ours. yours. theirs.	It's They're	Mike's. Carol's. Mike and Carol's.

a Read the information about two students, Mike and Carol, and match the objects with their owners.

Carol lives by the seaside. She goes to school on the school bus. She wears a uniform. She likes playing sport. She plays in the school tennis team.

Mike doesn't wear a uniform. He cycles to school every day. He likes windsurfing and listening to music in his free time. He also likes working on his computer. He plays football.

b Work in pairs. Check with your partner.

❝Whose tennis racket is it?❞

❝I think it's Carol's.❞

c Work with a new partner. Test each other.

❝Is the bicycle pump Carol's?❞

❝No, it isn't hers. It's Mike's.❞

LEARNING TO LEARN

5 **TALKING TO YOURSELF**

a Read what these students say about speaking English.

> I don't speak English very often. My English isn't very good and I don't like making mistakes. I feel stupid.

> I know that I make a lot of mistakes when I speak. But this isn't the most important thing. I think people can usually understand me. This is more important.

> When I was a child, I got a bicycle for my birthday. I got on the bike and started riding. I fell off the bike sometimes. But that's how I learned to ride. It's the same with learning English. I want to be able to speak English well so I speak English as much as I can.

> I want to speak good English. I don't like making mistakes. I want someone to correct all my mistakes.

b How do you feel about speaking English? Do you feel the same as any of the students? Which of the students have the most positive attitudes? Discuss your answers with your classmates and your teacher.

6 **a** Now read what the students say about practising their speaking outside school.

> I imagine that I am with an English friend. I talk English to my friend.

> I practise my vocabulary. I try to remember groups of words - colours, the months of the year - and say them aloud.

> I've got an Australian penfriend. I record my letters to her on cassette.

> I talk to myself. For example, I talk about what I did yesterday, I talk about what I can see, I talk about myself. I talk about anything and everything.

b Do you think the ideas are useful? Do you use any of these ideas yourself?

7 **a** Work in pairs. Take turns to choose one of these topics. Talk about the topic for a minute. Did your partner make many mistakes? Could you understand your partner?
* my house
* the weather
* a foreign country
* my school
* food
* a famous person

b Practise talking about the topics to yourself at home. Then work with your partner again.

Write some more topics on cards. Choose one of your cards and practise talking to yourself. Try to talk to yourself during the school holidays. Choose a different card every day.
* myself
* my favourite sport
* what I'm going to do tomorrow

GAME

8 NOUGHTS AND CROSSES

Preparation

a Read the following questions. Can you answer them? The answers are all in this book!
1 What is Jamaica?
2 How do you spell *biblioteca* in English?
3 Who were Laurel and Hardy?
4 Where is the Royal Mile?
5 How many players are there in a netball team?
6 When did Biró die?
7 Why did Queen Isabella give Columbus money?
8 How long is a netball match?
9 Which famous writer was born in Stratford-on-Avon?

b Work in pairs. Prepare similar questions for different squares of the board. You will need about 5 questions for each square. You will find lots of ideas for questions in this book. Write the questions, with their answers.

1 Who ...?	2 What ...?
Who was Grandma Moses? (An American painter) Who wrote ...?	What language do they speak in Egypt? (Arabic) What equipment do you need to play badminton ...?

Instructions

1 Play the game with another pair of students. Decide which pair is the 'Noughts' team, and which pair is the 'Crosses' team.

Nought

Cross

2 In turns, choose a square and answer a question.

" A question for square 5, please. "

3 When you answer a question correctly, write your team's symbol (a nought or a cross) on that square.

4 When your team has its symbols on three squares in a row, your team gets 1 point. You can get three squares in a row like this:

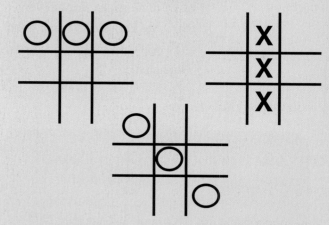

Remember: You can only have your team's symbol once on any square.

5 The game finishes when one pair of students has no more questions to answer. The winners are the players with the most points.

Now copy the board on a piece of paper and play the game.

1 Who ...?	2 What ...?	3 Which ...?
4 How many ...?	**5** How ...?	**6** How long ...?
7 When ...?	**8** Where ...?	**9** Why ...?

Did you enjoy the game? Prepare new questions and play it again.